I0568604

Second Edition

THE WAY I SEE IT

A Candid Review of Lessons from Life so far

PRISTINE
PRESS AND MEDIA

Joseph K. Chan

The Way I See It: A Candid Review Of Lessons From Life So Far

Library of Congress Control Number: 2014918554

ISBN
978-1-969642-39-5 (Paperback)
978-1-969642-38-8 (eBook)
978-1-969642-40-1 (Hardcover)

With all my love,

To my daughter, April; son-in-law, Joseph;

Grandsons Haven, and Pearce;

My son, Kevin; daughter-in-law, Marla;

Grandchildren Nathaniel, Betsy, and Caleb;

And

In memory of my dear wife, Liena

Contents

Preface

I was born with two rather restrictive birth defects. As soon as I was old enough to notice that I could not do some of the things other people could, I started asking why I had been given these obstacles. To have one of these defects was unfortunate; to carry the burden of two seemed very unfair.

As a little child, I didn't have an answer for myself. The family and the school system that I grew up in did not provide adequate support and guidance for children with special needs. I was only encouraged to measure up with my peers. That put a lot of stress on me. I worked hard to keep up, but no matter what I did, I was always below average in school. And the feeling of inferiority made me socially shy.

After I graduated from college and stepped into the workplace, my low self-esteem was a stumbling block. It was difficult to convince people to look beyond my obvious handicaps. One person who noticed my real potential was a woman I met at a workplace. We got married and had thirteen wonderful years together. She gave me understanding, encouragement, and patience. But our relationship did not last as long as I wanted—her life was cut short by breast cancer.

On the surface, this is a sad story, but one big lesson I have learned from this opera is that I am the one who decides whether it is a sad story or not. If I were to let the events in my life make me a sad person, then I would lose the chance to harvest all other fruits that can be realized. My story is one of perseverance, love, and personal triumph over fate. It is from pain and suffering I learned the most valuable lessons.

This process has not only led to insights about the physical aspects of life but has also enticed me to develop my personal views of the spiritual purpose of human life, the question of God and faith. I have learned that where I stand in these existential questions is the guiding light and sets the course for the remainder of my time on earth.

Chapters 1–9 contain my personal history and the lessons I learned in coping with birth defects and tragedies. Chapters 10–13 are about lessons in the spiritual aspects of life. Lessons in both categories have been all important in my establishing a meaningful life for myself.

The intended readers of this book are members of my immediate family, other relatives, friends, associates, and anyone who is interested to read it. One note for the broader audience is that there is a lot of detailed information about my long family history and work experience in Chapters 1, 5, and 9. To assist every reader to go through the book without being overwhelmed by detailed personal history, each chapter is divided into topical headings to serve as an overview and quick reference.

I have found that one of the greatest joys in life is learning and becoming a better person in some ways, slowly but surely. I am not an expert in philosophy or a spiritual teacher. I am only a thinking person with some experience that is worthwhile to share with my readers. Although I am not seeking agreement with my points of view, since I am still a learning work in progress, I believe that this book may bring hope and inspiration to a broad audience.

In the second edition, I have expanded Chapter 12 to include certain significant events since the publishing of the first edition in 2014. Over the past several years, I have gone through new experiences and learned new lessons. Many changes are underway, both at my personal level and in the world at large. Increasingly, I realized that although the changes in the world are not in my control, I am in control of how I respond to these changes. The Coronavirus pandemic of 2019, also known as COVID-19, is one such example.

It started in late 2019 and became a world pandemic in just a matter of weeks. Unfortunately, by July 2020, the United States became one of the most affected countries with more than 4 million cases and 150,000 deaths. As researchers in many countries around the world are racing against time to come up with a vaccine, medical professionals are urging everyone to wear face masks, wash hands frequently, practice social distancing, and stay home as much as possible. One of the characteristics of this virus is that anyone can be a carrier without symptoms, and therefore, people should follow these safety measures, not only to protect oneself but also to protect others.

As a good citizen, I follow all these recommendations personally. Staying home has brought new meaning to my work. They are still being done but only in different ways. Thanks to the availability of technology, much of the work I am committed to do can be done online over the internet. One new project I embarked on that is particularly worthwhile during this shelter-in-place period of time is to publish a second edition of my book.

Ironically, this worldwide pandemic has restricted my activities in some ways but brought new purposes in others. I believe a number of events in the past several years are significant enough for updating my autobiography, and the appropriate place for them is Chapter 12.

Introduction

I retired from the Association of Bay Area Governments in 2009, after serving twenty-six years as its chief financial officer, in my sixty-first year on earth. This was the last job in my career. I worked a total of thirty-six years after graduation from college. At this momentous occasion, it is a good time to look back.

One important realization was that I must already be in, or very close to, the last one-third of my life. This is not a negative or sad point of view. Rather, looking at my past results in a deep sense of gratitude and accomplishment, from how I dealt with the burden of birth defects as a child to my perseverance over bad odds to my accumulation of knowledge and insights. It has been a difficult but wonderful journey. I want my last one-third to be the most significant third, in terms of continued learning and growing and giving back to society with what I have learned and built up.

I was born with not one but two rather restrictive birth defects. The first is a genetic eye disease known as retinitis pigmentosa (RP). I have lived with low vision since childhood, and this eye disorder is progressive with age. Fortunately for me, my vision is relatively stable and did not decline noticeably until after age fifty. The second birth defect I had to learn to live with is paroxysmal kinesigenic dyskinesia (PKD), an involuntary muscular spasm brought on by other sudden movements, such as standing up from a sitting position, being startled, or reacting to a need to make a quick step. Attacks usually last less than a minute and do not involve loss of consciousness.

One neurologist told me that it is likely that the PKD is somehow tied to the RP. RP is known to come with other disorders. In my case, this is what I was given. Unlike RP, the PKD I have is not progressive. It reduced in frequency after age forty and gradually became, for the most part, under control. But it can still happen. I just have to be careful in taking care of myself; exercising and getting enough rest are helpful.

Growing up with low vision was a big challenge. Everything took longer to do. My reading speed was about half the normal speed, and I was barred from any sport that involved catching a ball and from driving a car. It has limited me socially too because I can't see well in dimly lit social gatherings. The main difficulty with the PKD is the embarrassment it causes when the attacks happen before people, and they often have. This is something very few people understand, and it is so difficult to explain.

Dealing with vision impairment as a child was difficult enough. Having muscular spasms in addition was a tremendous burden, of course. It seemed so unfair to have such a disadvantaged beginning. That was the feeling during my early years. My childhood was difficult, not only because of the need to develop special skills to cope with the birth defects; there also was an even bigger challenge resulting from the stigma about disabilities.

A physically challenged child needs special guidance to develop his or her full potential, and this guidance was lacking in the early part of my life. My parents were educated and responsible people, but through no fault on their part, they did not have the knowledge or experience to raise a special child. And so I was taught that these birth defects were handicaps. They were very undesirable, and the way to deal with them was to try to be normal and measure up with other people. This kind of upbringing actually produced a lot of fear and a sense of inferiority.

In the family where I grew up, feelings were not discussed. We could talk about everything else; but when someone expressed feelings, it was usually perceived as exaggeration, inappropriateness, or weakness. Growing up in a family of six, I felt lonely and was under a lot of stress. I didn't understand why I had been given these physical challenges, and no one around me was in the position to give me the guidance I needed.

In my childhood and early adulthood, I had to cope with not only low vision but low self-esteem as well. With all these odds stacked against me, I could have been defeated or depressed all my life. That is not the way it turned out. My story is one of personal struggle and triumph over fate. I am not saying that I haven't experienced defeat or depression. This has been a long learning experience, with sweat, blood, and tears produced in the process of becoming who I am today.

One important factor that prevented me from sinking to the bottom is that circumstances forced me to think about survival. I didn't want to be defeated or put into a box. Despite significant self-doubt, I worked hard to catch up. This struggle led to a number of useful skills that helped me complete my college education and start a career in accounting. What I did not expect was that this personal struggle would teach me much more than mere survival skills.

Over the years and decades, I have examined and developed insights on some of the most perplexing issues such as the purpose of life and the existence of God, suffering, faith, and love. I am now confident about where I stand with these big life issues, confident without being rigid or settled. In fact, I consider myself still a beginner, a work in progress reaching out to that enlightened consciousness in which there are no graduates.

At this point, when about two-thirds of my life has passed, I feel satisfied that I have done the best I could with all the adversities that were thrown at me, and overall, I am happy with the outcome. I want to document this very special journey, not only what happened but also how it made me feel, who helped me, how I achieved what I did, and the knowledge and insights I have accumulated so far. What I can promise you is that I will be candid in writing this book, telling my story in my own words and the way I see it.

You may not agree with some of my points of view, and what worked for me may not work for everybody. I don't intend to seek anyone's agreement or accuse anyone of wrongdoing. Although I don't intend to offer advice or solutions for others, it is my hope that my experience may encourage some people to develop their own insights and solutions.

1

Family History: The Family Tree

My father passed away in 1998, at the age of eighty-five. One very worthwhile project he did during his final years was writing a brief summary of the Chan family history. As I understand, he gathered the information from his personal notes and records obtained from our native village in China. It is an impressive family history—a total of 140 generations, spanning more than 4,000 years. This is certainly a record to be proud of.

Although it is necessary to begin my memoirs with this family history, presenting all the branches of this family tree would be beyond the scope of my book. Basically, I am listing in this chapter some of the known names and events in the direct line before me and more detailed stories of the most recent three generations, from my great-grandfather to my parents. I believe this long family history presents some intriguing insights into the importance of genealogy and provides the background for my own life story in the other chapters of this book.

ANCESTRY IN NORTHERN CHINA

The record began with the tribal king Huang Di (Yellow Emperor), 黄帝, who lived around 2600 BC when tribes began to settle on the banks of the Yellow River, 黄河. Eight generations from him, the record shows another tribal king, Shun (舜帝). Twenty-eight generations later, Wu Wei Mun (胡嬀滿) was appointed governor of the Chan District (穎川陳郡) in Henan Province (河南省) during the Zhou dynasty (周朝, 1122–225 BC). The word *Chan* (Cantonese) or *Chen* (Mandarin) means "old" or "aged." Nineteen generations after Wu, his descendant Chan Lai (陳厲) changed his last name to Chan, the name of the place he governed; this happened around 600 BC.

In the Chinese tradition, the last name or family name comes before the first name. Twelve generations after Chan Lai, his descendant Chan Sib (陳涉) participated in the uprising against the Qin dynasty (秦朝, 221–206 BC). Although Qin was the first dynasty to unite China and was credited with many achievements, including building the Great Wall of China, its first emperor, Qin Shi Huang (秦始皇), was oppressive to the people and ruled with tyranny. After his death in 210 BC, his son was quickly dethroned.

Eleven generations thereafter came Chan Sud (陳實), and five generations after him, Chan Deng (陳登) lived around the end of the Eastern Han dynasty (東漢, 25–220 AD). The Chan people stayed in northern China for another twenty-two generations, until Chan Huang Juen (陳洪進) moved south to the Fujian Province (福建省), probably during the Tang dynasty (唐朝, 618–907 AD).

From Yellow Emperor to Chan Huang Juen's father, there were a total of 105 generations spanning about 3,500 years. I would regard this period as ancient ancestral history, and some of the dates in this period are rough estimates.

SETTLEMENT IN SOUTHERN CHINA

Chan Huang Juen and his family flourished in the Fujian Province. His son was Chan Hu Yung (陳瑚翁), and seven generations after him came Chan Ng Yen (陳吾仁). His son Chan Fai Yung (陳輝翁) was appointed court advisor (諫議大夫) by an emperor in the Southern Song dynasty (南宋, 1127–1279

AD). He fell out of favor later and was sent to the Guangdong Province (廣東省). Guangdong is a southern province and was regarded as a barbaric region at that time.

Chan Fai Yung had seven sons. Their first names were Mok (謨), Suen (宣), Ying (英), Hoi (愷), Yuen (閏), Tao (圖), and Yen (仁). Mok was the scholar in the family. He passed the imperial examination with distinction and was appointed chief of the Board of Punishment (刑部侍郎), a high judicial position in the government.

Mok led his six brothers and their families to settle around the basin of the Pearl River (珠江). Mok had four sons—Mun Seen (文詵), Mun Jun (文振), Mun Lung (文龍), and Mun Hey (文起). Mun Hey was a merchant in the Sun Tek District (順德), near Guangzhou (Canton City, 廣州市). He had two sons—Chun Ling (春靈) and Yek Ling (躍靈).

Chun Ling's son Sing Po (性甫) had three sons—Ping Bo (平波), Ping Jen (平荐), and Ping Tao (平儔). During the Yuan dynasty (元朝, 1279–1368 AD), Sing Po and his family moved to the Toi Shan District (台山縣). The generations from Chan Fai Yung to Chan Ping Bo were the first six generations that settled in the Guangdong Province.

Eleven generations after Ping Bo, his descendant Kok See (覺思) and his five sons settled in the Lin Far Don village (蓮花墊) in Toi Shan District, during the Qing dynasty (清朝, 1644–1911 AD). From Kok See to me are the ten most recent generations, as follows:

Sau Yue (秀裕)—one of Kok See's sons; settled in the Fung Yuen Ley village (逄源里), near the Lin Far Don village
Yick Wo (益和)
King Yuen (敬元)
Fet Choy (發彩)
Fook Yin (福賢)
Jun Leong (震良)
Mann Gee (文治)

Wing See (榮士)
Kai Luen (繼倫), Joseph (me)

I have an older brother, Kai Shing (繼丞), Louis, and two younger brothers Kai Fong (繼昉), Stephen, and Kai Kwong (繼光), Anthony. For these recent generations, I am presenting mainly my direct line. Recording the siblings in each generation would probably take up a dedicated book.

FAMILY HISTORY SINCE MY GREAT-GRANDFATHER (1857–PRESENT)

Most of my ancestors were farmers, and they all lived in China until my great-grandfather, Jun Leong (震良, 1857–1907). He was the first in my family to come to the United States. He arrived in San Francisco in 1872 at age fifteen. In those days, people came by sailboats. Instead of going straight across the open ocean, they sailed close to land, stopping at many ports of call and doing trades along the way. Therefore, the one-way journey took several months. Many people from Guangdong Province started to come to San Francisco around that time, lured by the gold rush. In fact, San Francisco was nicknamed "Old Gold Mountain" by the early Chinese settlers. They did all kinds of labor work. As the Chinese population grew, a small Chinatown started to build up in downtown San Francisco.

A relative from Jun Leong's village accompanied him on the trip. However, when the ship arrived, they got separated. Not speaking a word of English, Jun Leong felt desperate as he stood at the pier and cried. A passerby took him to Chinatown. There he worked for thirty years in a restaurant on Maiden Lane near Grant Avenue. During his time in the United States, Jun Leong went back to China at least once. He got married and had only one child, my grandfather, Mann Gee (文治, 1881–1935). Jun Leong also brought his three younger brothers to the United States. In the early 1900s, he returned to China, bought some farmland near his village, and settled in for retirement. He didn't get to enjoy his retirement for long, though; he passed away around the age of fifty.

My grandfather, Mann Gee, was the only child and was raised by a very caring mother while his father was working in the United States. As a young man, he went into Chinese herbs retail and trading business in Hong Kong (香港). Apparently, his business was quite successful, enabling him to provide good education to his children. He sent his first son, Wing Gee (榮枝, 1902–1976), to the University of Michigan at Ann Arbor where he graduated with a degree in architecture. Wing Gee returned to Guangzhou and became well-known architect. His most famous architectural project was the AiQun Hotel Guangzhou (廣州爱群酒店). A fourteen-story structure completed in the late 1940s, it was the tallest building in southern China at that time. Preserved as a historical landmark, AiQun is still an operating hotel today.

My father, Wing See (榮士, 1912–1998), whose friends called him "Wings," followed his older brother's footsteps and also attended the University of Michigan–Ann Arbor and graduated with a degree in civil engineering in 1939. My father returned to Hong Kong from Michigan after graduation and tried to find work. By that time, Japan had invaded China, and the construction business slowed down as war escalated. He barely managed to make a living by doing odd jobs like painting houses.

My father was born in his native village, Fung Yuen Ley (逢源里). After he finished primary school at the age of eight, my grandfather brought him to Hong Kong to attend secondary school; and at thirteen, he was sent to Beijing (北京) to study Chinese literature. My grandfather believed that an education in the Chinese classics would improve my father's chances for a position in the government. After about two years, apparently, Beijing was not a suitable place for my dad. He finally completed his secondary schooling (high school) at the Ling Nan Middle School in Guangzhou. He then made a big move in 1935 to attend the University of Michigan in the United States.

My mother, Yu Shan Lan (余順蘭), Matilda (1921–2011), was born in Hong Kong. She grew up there with her parents and aspired to become a schoolteacher. After graduating from secondary school in 1939, she studied for the teaching certificate. Because her father and my grandfather were close friends, she met my dad at family gatherings when she was a little child. But they did not develop a friendship because my father was nine years older and he went to Beijing at the age of thirteen. They didn't get the chance to really know each other until after my father returned to Hong Kong from Michigan in 1939.

At that time, the surging war with Japan presented a very unsettling future for both of them. It was during that difficult period that they encouraged each other and developed a close friendship. In 1941, Japan invaded Hong Kong, and my father and mother decided to leave the war zone. They took with them a group of youngsters from both families and left Hong Kong by boat for their native place in the Toi Shan District in Guangdong Province. My mother's family lived in the Gut On (吉安) village, about half an hour's walk from my father's village, Fung Yuen Ley.

As they joined the fleeing refugees, my father and mother agreed not to get married during wartime because of the uncertainties. After they got settled in their villages, my mother found a job as a schoolteacher. Following some work opportunities, my father went to Kweilin (桂林) in Guangxi Province (廣西省). There he accidentally wandered into a US Air Force facility. He introduced himself and his civil engineering background and was hired on the spot by Col. Preston Brown, the commanding officer of the Air Force base in Kweilin.

At that point in the war, the US Air Force needed to build airfields in the Kweilin region. My father worked for the US Air Force building airbases in various locations in Guangxi Province until the war ended in 1945. He found work not only for himself but also for his older brother Wing Gee, his younger brother Wing Sik (榮錫), and many relatives from his village, who came to Kweilin and worked on his construction projects, as building airbases required a big labor force.

My mother held many teaching jobs in various parts of Guangdong Province during the war as she moved around seeking shelter in safe places. She and my father did not see each other during the war and kept in touch only by sending letters. Those several years were no easy time for my parents. They were eyewitnesses to the atrocities of war. They survived many bombing raids, watched Japanese soldiers murdering civilians, saw people starving to death, children being abandoned by the roadside after their parents were killed, and so many other horrific tragedies. That is what my parents' generation lived through.

Japan surrendered in August 1945, and the war ended. People scrambled to find lost relatives as they tried to put their lives back together. Colonel Brown, who was a pilot, gave my father a free ride on a military plane to Guangzhou. My dad could not travel with the masses because he had with him a suitcase full of cash, some of the payments for his work with the US Air Force. At that time, all business transactions had to be settled with cash because banks were still closed. My parents reunited in Guangzhou, and they got married in December 1945. Colonel Brown and my parents became lifelong friends. He and his wife were invited to my parents' fiftieth wedding anniversary party held in San Francisco in December 1995, and Colonel Brown made a speech at the celebration.

With the money he earned in Guangxi, my father and his two brothers, Wing Gee and Wing Sik, started a construction company. He bought an apartment building with several units and with a storefront on the ground floor. The ground floor was used as offices for the construction company, and the three brothers and their families lived upstairs. There was a boom in construction after the war, and business was good for my father's company.

The company took on a couple of notable projects. One was repair and expansion of the Guangzhou (Baiyun) Airport (廣州白雲機場), one of the major airports in southern China. The other was the construction of a residence for the widow of the late Dr. Sun Yat-sen (孫中山), the leader of the revolution that toppled the Qing dynasty and the first president of the Republic of China. After the war, the Nationalist Party decided to build a residence for his widow to commemorate Dr. Sun, the father of the republic. That house was built in Dr. Sun's native village and is probably preserved as a historical site still today.

This prosperity did not last long for the Chan clan. In 1948, the Communist Party was gaining power in China and took over Guangzhou in 1949. The Nationalist Party retreated to Taiwan. For a short while, the communists were friendly to the civilians, but very quickly the persecutions began. It was the have-nots against the haves. People were put on trials by mobs. They were humiliated, tortured, or put to death. Many people committed suicide under the oppression. Because my father worked for the US military, he knew he would be a target.

My parents decided to escape to Hong Kong, a safe haven under British rule. They had to leave inconspicuously, basically bringing just a small suitcase. In February 1950, my mother left first with a servant and the three of us—my older brother Louis, three years old; me, two years old; and my younger brother Stephen, four months old. We went from Guangzhou to Macau and then took a boat to Hong Kong. Macau was a Portuguese colony and shares a border with Guangzhou. This was a longer route but presented less risk of being caught.

With the help of some generous relatives in Macau, the five of us arrived safely in Hong Kong. With the small amount of money she had with her, my mother rented a small bedroom as our first dwelling place, and dinners were served on top of the one and only suitcase we had brought with us. Very fortunately, my mother found a teaching job at the Precious Blood Girls' Middle School within a week through a connection with her good friend Jenny Tong, who was teaching at that school. My father followed a few months later so that he could finish a construction project in progress.

My parents gave up everything they had built in Guangzhou to start all over again in Hong Kong, but they were happy to escape with their lives and their three young children. It took my dad several years to find a good job in his profession. To make ends meet, my mother took up a second teaching job at night. The first couple years were very difficult for us. We shared part of a house that had no toilet facility with two other families. We little kids were not old enough to notice the bleak circumstances, but it must have been very uncomfortable for my parents. It took four years for my parents to save enough money to buy their own place for us. Finally, in 1954, we moved into a flat on the ground floor of a building that my father's company had built. That was a huge improvement in living conditions.

My youngest brother, Anthony, was born in 1954. My father's business continued to do well, and in 1960, we bought a condominium unit on the top floor of a high-rise building with a view overlooking the beautiful Hong Kong harbor. It is important to note that such progress would not have been possible without my mother's hard work. She continued her teaching career until we immigrated to the United States in 1969.

Also, the servant my mother brought from Guangzhou, Ah Foon (亞寬), played an important role in helping my family through the difficult years. Because both parents had to work, she did all the housework and cooking and served as nanny for the four of us. During the 1960s, the communist factions in Hong Kong stirred up civil unrest with riots and bombing incidents. My parents didn't want to take any chances with the communists and decided to move to the United States. But this time, we were not desperate refugees. We bought properties in San Francisco, and my brothers and I attended various universities in the country.

WHY IS GENEALOGY IMPORTANT?

For one thing, it is certainly interesting to know who your ancestors were and to know their stories. Of course, we have a lot more information for the recent generations. My parents reestablished themselves to make a new livelihood three times in their lifetime, in Guangzhou, Hong Kong, and the United States. It was truly a remarkable story of perseverance, living through a brutal war and persecution with courage, risk-taking, and hard work. Looking farther back, my great-grandfather, Jun Leong, seemed to have a similar character—coming to the United States at age fifteen without knowing a word of English, all to make a better future for his family. Hats off to this spirit! They were truly pioneers.

I have written more about the most recent three generations only because I have more information about them from the stories I heard, mainly from my parents. I believe the people in each older generation had their challenges and difficulties too. They all had stories. Throughout China's long history, there have been so many dynasties and periods of warring states, and usually there were atrocities and economic unrest during changes of the ruling monarch. I can only imagine what some of my ancestors must have gone through.

From my point of view, as we recognize our ancestors' achievements, hard work, and triumph over adversities—it is important to note their failings and weaknesses as well. We know that if we don't learn from history, we may face the same tribulations again. My grandfather Mann Gee's contribution to future generations was his foresight to send his two oldest sons, my uncle and my father, to pursue university education in the United States. He would have provided the other sons good education too, had he lived long enough.

My grandfather had three wives. While he ran his herb-trading business in Hong Kong, he had two concubines. His first wife, my grandmother, was kept away in Fung Yuen Ley village. My grandfather had six children with his first wife, four with his second concubine, and three with his third concubine. So I have a total of four uncles and eight aunts, and I lost track of the number of cousins, some of whom I have never met. Polygamy was still a fairly common practice in China during my grandfather's days. It was regarded as a status symbol. It is hard to see whether it produced happiness in my grandfather's family. Obviously, some of his children did not get proper attention from my grandfather, and not every one of them did well in life.

Supporting such a big family must be a tremendous burden, and apparently, it adversely affected his health. He passed away at the age of fifty-four in 1935. A large part of the responsibility for supporting the younger siblings fell on the two oldest sons, Wing Gee and my father. My grandmother was truly a kind and generous woman. During the war, all the children of the concubines sought refuge in the village, and she provided them with accommodations and support.

Following my grandmother's example, my father treated the younger half brothers and half sisters as his siblings. That was a huge responsibility, and he carried it well. My father was an honest and upright person. He dealt with the customers of his construction business and his employees responsibly and fairly. However, he did have one weakness in the way he cared for his extended family.

In the construction company he started in Guangzhou after the war, he employed relatives to fill key management and subordinate jobs even though he knew some of them were not the right match for the positions. Consequently, the company had significant, inherent internal control issues. For example, my father knew there were wastes and inefficiencies in the operation. He had to keep an eye closed for the sake of preserving the relationships. Also, because my father, his two brothers, and their families were living in the apartments above the store, household expenses for the three families and operating expenses for the business were mixed. As a result, despite good business all year round, the company realized practically no profits. Such lack of distinction between family and business expenses and the inability to make changes would crumble the company eventually.

Looking back, even though my parents had to give up a booming construction business to start over from scratch in Hong Kong, it was a blessing in disguise. The communists dissolved a hopelessly corrupt company and forced everyone to make a fresh start. My two uncles and their families all escaped to Hong Kong as well and reestablished themselves like my parents did, but not in the same business. As it turned out, not living and working together was good for relationships in the extended family.

Apparently, my father did learn from the problems in his company in Guangzhou. After working as an employee for about ten years in Hong Kong, he started his own construction company with a couple of other partners who were not his relatives. He did not make a lot of money but made enough to support his family and send the four of us to college. Being able to rebuild his business again from the ground up in Hong Kong was certainly a great achievement.

As I finished writing the last paragraph, some second thoughts came to me. I have to be careful in judging my father's business operation from my point of view. I received my training in business administration here in the United States. The accounting and management practices were obviously very different back in my father's days in China. Although it is not possible for me to know his thoughts at that time, some observations can be made.

He came from a rural farming family, and farming in China back then was typically a family business. In a village, everyone is related, and that is the only kind of labor force available. That was my father's background. Furthermore, he started his company in Guangzhou right after the war ended, and everyone was looking for work at that time. News spread quickly in our village that Uncle Wing See had jobs. I can see the cultural and circumstantial factors compelling my father to employ so many relatives. Under such circumstances, even if I had been there back in 1945 to help him set up his company with all the knowledge and skills I have today, the outcome might not have been much different. Because I wasn't there at that time and what I know is not the whole story, it is always very difficult to judge history. All I can say is that there were both positive and negative consequences to how my father's company was run.

On one hand, he did establish a prosperous business and created many employment opportunities for his extended family. On the other hand, the lack of sound management policies fostered wastes and inefficiencies, and they grew like viruses in the organization. It didn't take long for the negative consequences to overcome the positive ones. Learning from history is a complex matter. It calls for understanding the cultural and circumstantial backgrounds behind the stories as we analyze their impacts on future generations. Personally, I believe it is very worthwhile to study the lives of past generations so that we may preserve their virtues and avoid the same painful consequences in our lives.

One other benefit we can derive from studying family history is the realization that every generation has its special challenges. In fact, every person's life is challenging in many different ways. Looking back on my own life story, there were cultural and circumstantial factors that played a part in the paths I took and the choices I made. I too have a long story and many lessons learned. My story is not over yet, but I believe it is important at this juncture to review my past, what I would like my future to be, and the legacy I want to leave behind.

2

What Was Given

I was born on January 7, 1948, in Guangzhou (Canton City), China. My family moved to Hong Kong in 1950. At that time, the Communist Party was prosecuting business owners and intellectuals. Their tactic was to put people on trial by mobs with no legal process. In view of what was coming, my parents decided to escape before the communists could get to them.

My brothers and I grew up in Hong Kong. My birthday on all my legal papers is January 7, 1949. Birth certificates were not issued in China back then, and because I wasn't doing well in school in the beginning, my parents changed my birthday to give me an extra year to catch up. As I mentioned previously, I was born with two restrictive birth defects—retinitis pigmentosa (RP), a genetic eye disease, and paroxysmal kinesigenic dyskinesia (PKD), a muscular spasm disorder. This is how my story began; the family I was born into and the birth defects have had a profound impact on my life.

RETINITIS PIGMENTOSA (RP)

RP is a group of inherited diseases characterized by night blindness and progressive loss of vision. In some cases, people with RP may not have other affected relatives. I don't know of other cases within the last three generations of my family. RP is progressive, and the rate of progression varies. Some affected people become totally blind in their thirties or forties, some become blind as children, and others may have some vision throughout their lives. Fortunately for me, the progression in my case has happened very slowly.

The decline in my vision was not noticeable until I was in my fifties. Because of the slow rate of progression, I hope to have some vision for the rest of my life. My reading speed was about 50 percent of normal when I was in school and for most of my working career. There are blind spots in my retina, in the form of a donut. So I can see in the center and on the sides, but not in between. Because of this condition, I cannot play any sport that involves catching a ball or drive a car. It has affected me socially too. I cannot participate well in dimly lit parties, and sometimes I am slow to react when people try to shake hands with me because I don't see the hand that is being held out to me.

Currently, there is no effective medical treatment for RP. Studies have shown that daily intake of vitamin A helps to slow the progression of vision loss. I have used other techniques to preserve my eyesight such as wearing sunglasses, using a magnifying glass to read small print, and taking breaks when my eyes feel tired. Maybe that is why the progression in my case has been as slow as it is. Whether I will become totally blind depends on two factors—the rate of progression going forward and how long I live.

Many research initiatives on RP are currently underway in various countries. Future treatments may include retinal gene therapy, transplants, artificial retina implants, stem cells, nutritional supplements, and drug therapies.

PAROXYSMAL KINESIGENIC DYSKINESIA (PKD)

PKD is a disorder in the brain that causes erratic involuntary muscular movements precipitated by sudden change in surroundings, such as the ring of a telephone, being startled, or standing up too quickly from a sitting position. The attacks usually last about half a minute, with no lapse in consciousness. This is the main difference between PKD and a seizure. There is no pain during the attacks, although the movements may cause me to bump my head or hands on surrounding objects. Also, if it happens while I am swimming, it may bring on cramps. I generally try to avoid going into deep water even though I am a good swimmer.

There is little warning before the attacks. Usually, right before an attack, there is a sensation like standing on a high place. One neurologist told me that my PKD is related to RP, which is known to associate with other brain disorders such as deafness and mental retardation. In my case, the associate disorder is PKD.

From my recollection, I began having PKD attacks after I started school, around age six or seven. The trigger, I believe, was stress brought on by restricted vision. Soon after I started kindergarten, I realized I couldn't participate in certain activities with other kids because of my low vision. As I began to feel disadvantaged, occasionally, other kids picked on me as being slow or clumsy. It was this kind of psychological pressure that brought out the PKD that was predisposed in me, waiting for a prompt.

The PKD attacks increased in frequency and intensity during my teenage years to probably about once a week, as I attempted to balance biological growth and academic and social requirements. A mild attack may not be noticeable to the people around me. When the strong attacks come on, I can't even stand up. I have to crouch or kneel or sit. The movements are so severe that my eyeglasses may fall off, and I may sustain cuts and bruises. The intense attacks were most frequent during my teenage years, were sustained in my twenties, and gradually declined after I turned forty.

There are a number of drugs that can help reduce the frequency of PKD attacks. I was prescribed Elavil and Dilantin.

These helped control the attacks but did not prevent them. I could still have an attack if startled by a sudden need to make a quick stand or step. Other factors that may make me more vulnerable to attacks are fatigue, not having enough sleep, or having a cold. Because PKD carries a psychological burden, therapy can help. For a short period of time in my early twenties, I received professional counseling. In dealing with any disease, knowledge is the key. The knowledge of what the disease is helps a lot in addressing the emotional part of it.

WHAT IS IT LIKE TO LIVE WITH A COMBINATION OF RP AND PKD?

The main difficulty with RP is the slow reading speed and exclusion from certain activities. I had to learn special skills and adopt alternative ways of doing things. One of the most difficult aspects of living with PKD is the embarrassment it brings and having to explain to people what it is. Most people don't have any exposure to this rare disease. It is estimated that the rate is about 1 case out of 150,000 people. I haven't yet met another person with PKD. RP, on the other hand, affects 1 out of 4,000 people. What is the occurrence rate for a combination of both RP and PKD? I have not been able to find any published information specifically about such a combination. Obviously, it is extremely rare.

Dealing with both disorders was a tremendous physical and emotional burden in the process of growing up from a child to an adult. Of course, I have asked the "why me?" question. It is a natural reaction when you compare yourself with others and find that you are not the same, and so you ask why you are not like everybody else. This question can lead a person to despair or depression, especially when the subject matter is a birth defect. There is absolutely nothing I did to cause these birth defects or make me deserve them. They were just simply given to me. Is it unfair? This is a lifelong question and can be answered in many ways.

It seems about half of my energy has been consumed by dealing with the challenges of RP and PKD. In my young years, I was preoccupied with learning survival skills. It was a long, difficult process for me to develop the skills and self-confidence necessary to be an independent and productive person. One factor that kept me going might have been a need deep down to make the best out of it all. Apparently, there was also tenacity in me, as I refused to accept defeat as early as my teenage years. I worked very hard to catch up with and please others. Slowly but surely, I made progress, and that made me always curious about my potential.

My major health issue today is declining eyesight due to the progressing RP. The PKD has mostly subsided and is no longer a threat; as long as I maintain good physical shape, it should remain under control. RP has been progressing noticeably over the past several years to the point that I now can hardly see faces clearly in a conversation. And I have to walk with a cane to avoid bumping into things even in sunlight. It feels like my eyesight is closing down on me.

Should I worry about becoming totally blind? First of all, I am already very fortunate in the sense that many people who have RP become blind at age thirty to forty. I have had limited eyesight for much longer than expected and have done a lot with it, and I had plenty of notice about the progressive nature of RP.

Another point of view is that the progression of RP is not as threatening as other progressive diseases such as cancer, Alzheimer's, and Parkinson's. In comparison with the diseases some people I know are going through, mine is not so bad. I also want to draw from the people in my ancestry as presented in chapter 1 and the challenges they faced in their lives. What do all these dead people have to offer? A lot! If not for their perseverance, I wouldn't even be here. They paved the way for me in genes and spirit. Even though most of their stories have not been documented, I can imagine there must be many unsung heroes in all the generations that came before me.

Looking back at how far I have come, it has been an incredible journey. Despite the difficulties they have caused, RP and PKD did not impair my intellectual abilities. On the contrary, they enticed me to think and struggle for answers. What was also given to me, although I didn't realize it during my early years, was the insight that life is an opportunity to understand the universal truths and to decide what to do with new knowledge. This has been the motivation for me to document in a book the lessons I have learned so far. This is one of the best ways to share and pass on knowledge and insights.

I wish I knew more about the lives of some of the remarkable people in my long family history and the lessons they learned. That, too, is motivation for me to write an autobiography, not because my story is more worthwhile to write than theirs, but because I have some tools they didn't have—a personal computer and access to the internet, tools that are invaluable for a book project. I feel that it truly is a blessing to have such an opportunity.

3

My Childhood: My Earliest Memories

In February 1950, when I was two years old, my family moved from Guangzhou to Hong Kong, and that is where my memories begin. I was too young to remember my birthplace. It was a bold and risky decision my parents made to escape the communists' persecution. It must have been a very painful choice to give up the good life they had established, but there were not too many options. It was the right decision.

We escaped with our lives for a new beginning in Hong Kong. My parents did not have time to liquidate their assets, and basically, we brought with us a suitcase and the clothes on our backs. We left in Guangzhou everything my parents had built up since the end of World War II.

Our first dwelling place in Hong Kong was a bedroom at the back of a flat that we shared with another family. We slept on boards placed on top of a few stools, and the suitcase we had brought served as our first dining table. When one of my father's loyal former contractors built a dining table for us with his own hands, we were overjoyed to receive such a gift. It was a wooden table with two folding leaves, perfect for our cramped quarters. I still remember that dining table because my brothers Louis and Stephen and I spent a lot of time playing underneath it.

That was our playground in that tiny bedroom.

URBAN VILLAGERS

After living in that cramped space for about a year, we moved to a refugee settlement, a ghetto with wooden sheds and stone houses. The house we rented was a small two-level stone structure. We were on the ground floor, which had three bedrooms, but we were sharing the unit with two other parties. One of them was my mother's older sister Janet, her husband On-Mann Leong, and their son Bennett. They lived in the front bedroom. Three young construction workers shared the middle bedroom. We took the bedroom at the back. There were no living and dining rooms, only a straight hallway outside the bedrooms running from the front door to the backyard.

An L-shaped concrete patio wrapped around the front part of the house. The kitchen was behind our bedroom, facing a small backyard. Also in the backyard was the only restroom; it was about the size of a closet, with no flushing toilet. In the middle of it was a holding tank. You didn't go near that restroom unless you really had to. It was very stinky. Every day, a sewer collection service came by to empty the tanks for all the houses in that neighborhood.

There was no bathroom in the house. Everyone took baths in the kitchen with a bucket of water. Cooking was done over firewood, which took a long time to light and produced a lot of smoke. The walls inside the kitchen were blackened, and it was not a very pleasant place. There was electricity, but we didn't have a refrigerator. Buying fresh groceries at markets close by was a daily routine. Laundry was done by hand and drip-dried on the front patio. When it rained, we had laundry hanging inside the house.

The community was an urban village right behind a busy street and at the foot of a hill. Dirt roads and narrow alleys ran between the houses. Behind this community was a stone mine farther up the hill. Explosives were used in the excavating operation. Every day, before the explosives went off, someone beat a gong to warn the residents. Right next to the entrance of the village was a police station and academy with a courtyard outside the facility. I liked to watch the marching and training activities of the police cadets with their full gear on.

We little kids were not bothered by the overcrowded and unsanitary accommodations. Actually, life in the village was a lot of fun for us. There were many children among the households. We played hide-and-seek, hiked up the hill, dug up earthworms, looked for tadpoles in the creek, flew kites, and were creative in coming up with all kinds of games. During the midautumn festival, all the kids in the village came out with their lanterns at night. That was one festival we always looked forward to.

The people who lived there were poor but decent. I don't remember any crimes when we were there. We were also too young to know how difficult it was for our parents to provide for the family. My father couldn't find a well-paying job for the first three years in Hong Kong. During that time, my mother took on two teaching jobs and was just barely able to make ends meet. Around 1951, my father learned that the US military was planning to expand certain facilities in one of the Pacific islands. Thinking that his work with the US Air Force in Guangxi might give him an advantage in this opportunity, he borrowed some money from his brother-in-law C. F. Wong, the husband of his sister Yet Ha, to make a trip there.

Upon his arrival, he was disappointed to learn that a contractor had already been engaged for the project. Not only he did not get any work; he incurred a debt. Despite this setback, he came home carrying some toys for us kids. I remember the day when he came home from his trip.

Finally, in 1953, my father got a job as a salesman in a home appliance store. That was not what he was trained for, and it was a low-paying job. He did that for about a year before he was offered an engineering position in a construction company. That was a turning point for our family. In late 1954, we moved into a flat on the ground floor of a newly constructed building in the city. My father received it as part of his compensation for that construction project. It was the first property we owned in Hong Kong.

We lived as urban villagers in that refugee community for almost four years. Those years of experiencing village life and nature were significant to us little kids.

A TRAGEDY AND A BLESSING

Life is never a straight line. In 1952, my mother gave birth to my sister Mary. My parents were overjoyed because they had three boys and had wanted a girl. Unfortunately, Mary lived only nine days. Apparently, she was born with a defective heart. She didn't have a chance with the medical technology in the early 1950s. I have only a faint memory of her because I was only four years old. But this memory stayed with me. Even though she had such a short life, she made an impact. She was loved and missed. I remember my mother cried.

From my point of view, no life is pointless. Even though it may be difficult to see, there is a purpose in everything. My parents decided to try for another pregnancy, but they got another boy. My youngest brother, Anthony, was born in 1954. He was a beautiful and healthy baby and very cute. We all were so happy to have him.

STARTING SCHOOL

From the time I was a baby, my parents had noticed that I had difficulty seeing. As I was approaching school age, they took me to an eye specialist for an assessment. After his examination, the eye doctor told my parents that I might not be able to attend school. When we came home, my father cried. He said to my mother that it seemed so unfair; he had been a good person, generous to family and other people, and couldn't understand why he had been given a child who could not be educated. My mother was more positive and thought that they should let me try to see how much I could do.

I started kindergarten in 1954. My eyesight didn't present a problem in the beginning because the activities in kindergarten were mostly singing, drawing, and artwork, with little reading and no homework. In the following year, I entered first grade at the Holy Cross School. As reading and homework increased, my vision started to give me difficulty. My reading speed was slow to begin with, and my eyes got tired quickly under strain. I had to take frequent breaks, and so I needed extra time to do homework. Seeing the blackboard in the classroom was a problem. I had to sit in the front row. Even so, I usually had barely enough time to copy the notes on the blackboard before the teacher erased them.

I soon learned that I also had difficulty with activities on the playground—for example, playing chase with other kids or catching a ball. Pretty soon, I was excluded from these activities. And I was called names such as "elephant" and "clumsy," not only by kids but also by adults. People generally didn't have a vicious intent and thought it was funny. I remember once a teacher said to me in front of the whole class, "You are number one when it comes to clumsiness!" The whole class laughed. This comment was seared into my memory. How other people looked at me bothered me a lot; it was hurtful.

I didn't get much support at home either. My parents' main focus was making sure that we kids studied hard and got good grades. Regarding my being called "clumsy," my parents' attitude was that this observation was correct, and they did not have the knowledge and experience to help me deal with it. The adults around me had no idea how heavy a burden it was on me emotionally. I was scared and embarrassed about myself. And since no one seemed to understand, I bottled all those feelings inside me.

I believe it was around that time, at about age seven, that I began having PKD attacks. PKD is a disorder in the brain that is very likely associated with my vision disorder. No one really knows the exact biological explanation for it. Our knowledge of how the human brain works is still very limited. Apparently, I was born with a predisposition to have muscular spasms that can be triggered by emotional stress. These episodes of muscular spasm increased in frequency and intensity throughout my teenage and adult years and gradually subsided after age forty.

Usually, the attacks came on when I was startled by something near me, when I stood up too quickly from a sitting position, or when I was stressed by the volume of homework assignments. The attacks involved involuntary muscular movements of my face, hands, and legs. The mild episodes might not have been noticed by the people around me, but when the strong ones came on, I couldn't even stand up. There was no pain or loss of consciousness during the attacks, but I could sustain cuts and bruises if my head or hand hit some hard objects around me.

The most difficult aspect of this disease was the embarrassment it caused. The psychological burden was terrible. I had no idea what caused the attacks and why I had been given such a burden. My parents were saddened by it and worried about me. They brought me to see medical specialists, and I was prescribed medications. The treatments were not significantly effective, and I still had occasional attacks. The combination of impaired vision and muscular spasms was a monstrous obstacle as I was trying to develop social skills. I felt inferior, and my self-confidence was low for a very long time.

Despite the problems with my eyesight and my nerves, one sport I was quite good at was swimming, although I had to be careful not to go into deep water. I could also participate in some group games—those that depended on memory. I did want to play with other kids as much as I could, and I did make some friends. In fact, I tend to keep friends for a long time. I have a few lifelong friends. One of them is my second grade classmate Vincent Kwong, who became an environmentalist. He is now retired and lives in Toronto, Canada, with his wife.

THE STRENGTHS AND WEAKNESSES OF MY FAMILY

My parents were hardworking, educated, and decent people. They were conservative but willing to take risks if they had to. In fact, as my family history presented in chapter 1 suggests, perseverance seems to be a characteristic handed down through the generations.

My parents provided us with good education, food, and shelter. However, one weakness in this well-provided environment was the lack of guidance for dealing with my physical handicaps. There appeared to be a stigma associated with birth defects, which were seen as bringing shame to the family. The way to handle these disorders was to do the best you could to hide them from other people by trying to be normal and measure up with others.

Another weakness in my family was that expression of feelings was not encouraged. We could talk about homework, the economy, and world affairs. But deep feelings such as fear and anger were generally suppressed. Partly due to the Chinese culture, I was supposed to keep negative things to myself. Such an environment put horrendous stress on me as a physically challenged child. I felt very lonely even though I was surrounded by people.

WHAT I HAVE LEARNED FROM THESE FAMILY STRENGTHS AND WEAKNESSES

My family had much strength. Although we went through a period of hardship and poverty when we escaped from China to settle in Hong Kong, it didn't take too long for my hardworking parents to turn the situation around, and we were not lacking in material things. My family's weaknesses were in communication and emotional support. I learned later that these weaknesses are very common among many other families.

Lack of emotional support may lead to a number of mental health issues. Many of these families are well provided for by responsible parents, yet they produce children with emotional disorders that could last a lifetime. Most families want their children to be smart or have a high IQ, but most people know little about emotional intelligence, or EQ. For a productive life, EQ is just as important as IQ. We need EQ to feel positive while encountering adversities in life and to have healthy relationships with people.

My childhood was a struggle. I hated some of the negative perceptions of me. They hurt, and deep down, I knew I didn't deserve them. Perhaps this feeling of injustice gave me the motivation to fight back quietly, learning skills to compensate for my physical weaknesses. Despite my efforts, I was barely able to catch up. My grades in school were below average, and socially, I was shy. I was up against a general perception that I was either not very smart or not working hard enough. Although I was terrified as a child, I wanted to prove that I was not what some people might think. Apparently, my desire not to be put in a box was stronger than my fear of rejection.

Another factor that kept me going was that I saw how hard my parents worked. Even though I didn't get much emotional support from them, their intentions were good. I learned later in life that dealing with people's misperceptions about me would be a lifelong challenge. People are often misled by their own perceptions, myself included. The effective treatment for misperception is recognizing the truth. This may sound intuitive, but the truth can be very difficult to deal with or accept, especially when examining it may bring up guilt or shame. Fear of these feelings is probably one of the main causes of communication issues in families. Many people choose to ignore or deny fear and guilt and hope that they will go away, but that only perpetuates the issue.

It took decades for me to learn this—the truth is that there is nothing shameful about birth defects. They are fairly common and come in many different forms. If being physically challenged had made me a depressed or resentful person, I would not have been able to realize my full potential. What I can share from my own experience is that my handicaps actually elevated my curiosity about how the human body functions. The disorders have hurt me in some ways but have helped me develop in other ways. They contributed to my quest for knowledge, and I went very far with that quest, beyond the biological and physical aspects of my body to ponder the broader and deeper meanings of life.

It is true that each one of us is given a life that is like no other. The need to be the same as other people can lead to a number of misperceptions about the term *disability*. It is closer to the truth to acknowledge that each person is "differently able."

Willingness to acknowledge the truth is the foundation of learning. The truth may be painful, but that is where learning should begin. The physical challenges put an extra burden on my learning process, but as I made progress slowly but surely, that progress also generated an enormous curiosity about how far I could go.

Also, there are people around who are willing to listen and understand. Sometimes it may take some effort to find them. I have certainly come a long way to get to where I am today. The later chapters of this book review this very special journey.

4

Growing Up: My Secondary Education

Under the education system in Hong Kong when I was there, children attended primary school for six years starting at age six. Then they attended secondary school for five years. At the end of the fifth year, graduating students were required to take a public certification test. The results of this certification served as entrance qualification for university.

In 1959, I transferred from the Holy Cross School to enter primary 5 (fifth grade) at the Wah Yan College, a secondary boys' school run by the Irish Jesuits. Although Wah Yan was a secondary school, it started with the last two years of primary school back in 1959. Secondary school in Hong Kong is equivalent to a combined junior high and high school in the United States.

At that time, secondary education in Hong Kong was very rigid. Basically, everyone studied the same courses in each school year. There were no electives and very limited accommodations for students with special needs. I believe that there were schools for blind and visually impaired people. But I did not know about them, and besides, my parents still would have much preferred sending me to regular schools.

The school system in Hong Kong followed the British philosophy, which strives to screen out and educate the brightest people who are expected to take up leadership roles in society. Wah Yan College was one of the most prestigious secondary schools in Hong Kong. It was known for its academic standing. The subjects we studied included English literature, Chinese literature, English history, Chinese history, physics, chemistry, biology, geometry, algebra, trigonometry, physical education, and religion. We studied pretty much all these subjects every year.

Each class of 160 students was ranked by test scores and assigned to four rooms from A to D, about 40 heads in each, with the highest scores in room A and the lowest in room D. Students in rooms A and B were generally expected to be future scientists, engineers, and medical doctors. Those in rooms C and D were expected to go into arts, business, and other administrative fields.

WHAT I DIDN'T LIKE ABOUT THIS KIND OF SCHOOLING

This education system was very competitive, and test scores meant just about everything. With my slow reading speed, I could hardly keep up with the reading and homework for that many subjects. In addition, I often could not finish tests in the given time. The school did not have the means to provide me with test papers with large print, so I had to read with a magnifying glass, which slowed me down significantly. And so, I was in room C from the first year to the fourth and room D in my graduating fifth year.

The unwritten message from the school to us C and D students was something like "Work harder, kids." To me, personally, that kind of attempt at motivation was very insensitive. This system of classifying and segregating students based on test scores had significant impact on group behavior. It established two apparent social groups—AB and CD—and fostered misperceptions of superior and inferior capabilities of people. I felt very embarrassed to tell people which room I was in.

From my point of view, the biggest issue with such an education system is that society isn't divided up that way. When we leave school and go into the workplace, we have to interact effectively with people of different backgrounds and abilities. The overemphasis on science subjects was also out of touch with the real world. Society needs excellence in every specialty, with engineers, medical doctors, lawyers, accountants, artists, musicians, schoolteachers, stay-at-home parents, and so on.

MY EMOTIONAL BURDEN DURING SECONDARY SCHOOL

My secondary school did not help in enhancing my self-image. Schoolwork and homework drained my energy and made me physically tired. When I am tired, I am vulnerable to PKD attacks. It was during my teenage years I had strong PKD attacks most frequently. I remember one time I had a PKD attack in front of the whole class as I was making a presentation. I had PKD attacks while running after a bus, while walking along the hallway, and sometimes even when I was sitting still, listening to a lecture. Again, the most difficult aspect of PKD is the embarrassment it brings.

I couldn't explain to people what PKD is because I knew very little about it at that time, and it was so difficult to describe. My friends, teachers, and family were not in the position to help much beyond giving me their sympathy. My feelings during this period were a mixed bag. On one hand, I felt inferior and was timid before people; and on the other hand, there seemed to be a voice deep down that kept saying I was more able than what people might think. This was one of the main factors that kept me going, and as I made small progress, I felt an increasing curiosity about how much more I could learn and grow.

There was one Jesuit priest, Father McGovern, who said to me that I would overcome PKD when I got older. He was the only one who apparently had some knowledge about the disorder. I had two or three classes with Father McGovern. I kept what he said in my memory and hoped that he was right.

The sports we played in physical education classes were soccer, basketball, table tennis, and floor exercises. I basically had to sit out all the activities that involved eye-body coordination. All I could do was floor exercises. At that age, it was very important to be able to keep up with friends. Being excluded from most sports made me feel socially inept. I wished I could be a popular and active person like some of my classmates. Despite my limitations in certain activities, I gradually developed my own interests and explored activities suitable for me. I liked doing body workouts. As I grew, I became quite muscular, and actually, I liked how I looked.

Socially, I was quiet in school. I did participate in some religious group work such as visiting people. My mother was a Catholic, and my brothers and I were baptized before we finished primary school. I did not have wild or mischievous adventures like some of my classmates did. The only stunt I remember was making a trap with two other guys in the sandpit used for long-jumping by digging a hole and covering it with one sheet of newspaper and a thin layer of sand so that people would get a shoe full of sand when they stepped into it.

We watched from a distance and got a kick out of seeing our victims swear and curse. That was my idea. The other two guys were Vincent Kwong and John Suen. They both started primary 5 with me. John is now a professor at Cal State University in Fresno. He recently told me that he still remembers that stunt we did too.

A few other guys I still keep in touch with from the Wah Yan days are Ed Lai and Stephen Chan. Like Vincent and John, Ed started primary 5 in 1959 with me, and Stephen came in 1963. Ed, Stephen, and I later attended the University of Wisconsin. Ed lives in the Bay Area, and Vincent and Stephen settled in Toronto with their families. As I get older, it is great to have friends from high school days. We have great fun whenever we get together.

WHAT I LEARNED AT WAH YAN

It was during my very challenging secondary school years that I learned some valuable skills. Since it was not possible for me to catch up with all the reading, I learned to read selectively. For example, before I read into a chapter of a textbook, I looked at all the diagrams and the topical headings first to get an overall concept. I learned to highlight the key words and make notes. This worked well for technical subjects. Literature subjects could not be skimmed; they had to be read more thoroughly.

I also learned how to prioritize and focus on the essential subjects that I must pass in order to ascend to the next class. It is important for every teenager to keep up with friends. The challenges for me were the overwhelming volume of homework, difficulty with some of the sports, and participating in dimly lit social gatherings. I focused on academics as much as I could, and I did get through secondary school, barely passing enough subjects to graduate in 1966. My education up to that point had not given me good training in social skills and self-confidence. I had a lot to catch up when I entered the real world.

It seems that the most important lessons I got out of this period were how to work efficiently and not to take no for an answer. I knew that the stigma of my birth defects was unfair, and I believe that led to a strong desire to prove myself in some way. On the other hand, I did worry about how much headway I could make in the competitive real world where first impressions count a lot. Would someone look beyond my physical handicaps and give me a chance? That was the predominant question in my mind.

I realized that even though my grades were below average, they were the results of my best effort. What I did not appreciate fully at that time was that I did receive a broad education. I also learned to speak and write English quite well, thanks to the Irish Jesuits. These skills served me well throughout my life. The Irish priests who educated me were great people.

Each one of them had a distinguished personality, and I admired their devotion to their work. They also exposed me to the concept of God and the Bible. Although I wasn't a strong believer at the time, my curiosity about the truths of human life started back then. Just like my struggle in dealing with birth defects, my spiritual development was a hard struggle too. There is a long story about this process in the later chapters of this book.

MY INTEREST IN CLASSICAL MUSIC

There were a couple other developments during my teenage years that had a significant, lifelong impact on me. The first was my interest in classical music. It started with listening to a few records of classical music my father bought. I gradually developed a taste for classical music and began taking violin lessons at age fifteen. In retrospect, the violin might not have been the most suitable musical instrument for me.

Playing the violin requires not only a passion for music but also a body that is physically sound. With my muscular spasms, the guitar probably would have been easier for me. But I liked the sound of the violin, its closeness to the human voice, and the range of human emotions it could convey. Early on, I knew I wouldn't be good enough to be a performer, but I wanted to know as much as I could about the techniques for playing this instrument. Even though I cannot play like a professional violinist, I have learned enough to know what is good playing and to appreciate the great violinists.

Music actually provided me an emotional balance as I coped with my disorders. I am glad that I discovered music instead of getting involved with drugs, alcohol, or other destructive behaviors. Of course, I did not have the foresight at that time to consciously choose music as a hobby; I only stumbled upon it. I gradually learned over time that music gave me relief when I was sad or frustrated.

Music really is the language of the soul. It captures the full spectrum of human emotions, from joy to sadness. And most of the time, music conveys beauty. Even sad music can be beautiful, and beauty is a quality that is consistent even under bleak circumstances; it can be better felt than described in words. I have been really fortunate to have an appreciation for it.

NOTICING PEOPLE WITH PHYSICAL DISABILITIES

This was the second important development during my youth. During my teens or even younger, I saw people without arms or legs on the streets. I always wondered how it felt to live without a limb. I didn't try to talk to them because I was timid with people at that time. I didn't know what to say. Even so, these observations at a young age seemed to make a lasting impact on me—showing me that although my birth defects were very undesirable, there were people in worse shape than I was.

Although this realization did not ease the difficulties I was facing, it paved the way for me to develop empathy for others. Later in my career, my sensitivity to the feelings of people proved very helpful in managing an organization. The main function of management is getting things done through teamwork. And the ability to understand how people feel is the key in soliciting loyal and dedicated service from them.

FAMILY LIFE DURING MY TEENAGE YEARS AND ITS INFLUENCE ON ME

My father continued to do well in his construction business during the late 1950s. In 1960, we moved to a high-rise condominium building halfway up the Victoria Peak with a spectacular view of the Hong Kong harbor. I was twelve years old that year. The unit was rather small by American standards, about eight hundred square feet, but we were reasonably comfortable. It was by far the best dwelling place we had in Hong Kong, in comparison to our previous ones.

Our family life was busy for everyone. Both parents had full-time jobs. We kids were always busy with homework from school. To enable my parents to work full-time, we had a number of household helpers, including a cook, a housekeeper, and private tutors, to help us with homework. Our parents had really done their best to provide for us.

Occasionally, on weekends, the family went out for a movie or lunch. During the summer months, we went swimming quite often. We kids particularly looked forward to Christmas, when our parents took us shopping for our gifts. For Chinese New Year, our parents took us to visit relatives, and the adults gave us good-luck money in red envelopes. Each one of us could collect two to three hundred dollars over that holiday.

Because most of the uncles and aunts had moved to Hong Kong from China, we had many families to visit during Chinese New Year. My father's sister Yet Hah, her husband C. F. Wong, and their four children lived only a few blocks from us. The four of them—Esther, Earnest, Roberta, and Francis—and the four kids in my family were close in age. Esther, the oldest one, is a year younger than me. We got together quite often with them. There were many other cousins in the extended family. We had big parties during holidays and on special occasions.

A family that appears to be healthy can have hidden issues. The family I grew up in was caring, responsible, and well provided for but emotionally unsupportive and cold in some ways. Both of my parents were college educated. However, in my family, the one area of weakness was in the understanding of human emotions. In my upbringing, it was okay to express love and joy; but there was a lack of guidance on how to deal with fear, frustration, and anger. Because these feelings were usually regarded as inappropriate when they were expressed, over time, we just refrained from talking about them.

It was part of my family culture to keep up with others; and how others might look at us was, therefore, very important. My birth defects, for example, were things to be swept under the rug. We all have a tendency to avoid examining things that make us uncomfortable. This explains how prejudice can last for a long time and how a family can be caring but rigid or caring but cold.

It is human nature to seek pleasure and comfort. We usually avoid hardships until we are compelled to deal with them. In 2006, Al Gore produced the film *An Inconvenient Truth* to document how the environment on earth can be damaged by human neglect. This is another example of a subject matter that we need to know about, but it is not a popular topic to take on. In my case, I was nudged to learn about the emotional aspects of human behavior because the way I was treated as a child hurt me.

My upbringing gave me tremendous stress and low self-esteem. One might say I turned out quite well after all. Let me say that the way I turned out is an anomaly. I shouldn't have accomplished what I did starting out with the distorted self-image that was imposed on me as a child and teenager. Despite having a good formal education, I could have been a casualty in the real world. Throughout my career working in various organizations, I met so many people who had emotional problems from their personal backgrounds that impaired their ability to function in the workplace, and they fell by the wayside. Many of these emotional problems are signs of an injured self-image and can manifest as defensiveness, rage, or doing the minimum to get by.

I must point out here that I don't mean to diminish the importance of the formal education my parents worked so hard to give me. They provided for me to the best of their abilities and really didn't owe me anything else. It was my responsibility to make the best out of it. As a young adult, I couldn't benefit fully from my academic training because my self-image was constantly a burden, dragging me down. It was later in life, when my self-image was repaired, that I could appreciate the full value of a good education. My learning curve in becoming an upright and productive person was very long and involved factors, in addition to my family background and schooling.

MY COLLEGE EDUCATION

When I graduated from secondary school in 1966, my grades were not high enough to get me into any prominent university. I enrolled in the Hong Kong Baptist College, which was an unaccredited college at that time but became part of the Chinese University years later.

I started in the civil engineering department but quickly realized that my eyesight presented a challenge in reading intricate engineering drawings. In the second semester, I transferred to the accounting department. Many people who enrolled in this college did not intend to graduate from there because degrees from an unaccredited school were not valued highly in the job market. My goal too was to obtain a college degree elsewhere, from a university. Because of the limited number of universities and colleges in Hong Kong, there was an outflow of students seeking higher education overseas.

In 1968, I went to England to study accounting at the College of Further Education, in Worthing, Sussex. It was not a university, but I intended to go there and look for other opportunities. Soon after I settled in England, I realized that there was virtually no chance that I would gain admission to a university there. I went back to Hong Kong in 1969 and looked for a university in the United States.

At that time, several campuses in the University of Wisconsin were in the process of expanding their student diversity. As an incentive to attract foreign students, they were offering free tuition for the first year. I applied and was accepted by the University of Wisconsin–Whitewater. Because my grades in college were better than what I had received in high school, I was able to transfer some of the credits earned at the Hong Kong Baptist College and in England, and I entered my sophomore year at UW–Whitewater in September 1969. My parents migrated to the United States that year and made San Francisco our new home. Soon after I was admitted, I informed my high school buddy Stephen Chan about the opportunity at

UW–Whitewater, and he also transferred over from Hong Kong.

Getting into a university was a major milestone in my education. I wanted to earn a college degree that could lead to career opportunities. I continued to study business administration with a major in accounting. The business administration curriculum at Whitewater was good.

In addition to the major subjects, it included many practical courses such as business English, computer programming, psychology, economics, and business law. Computer programming, in particular, was a course I found very useful throughout my career. The understanding of computer software helped me implement accounting systems for a few organizations during my career. The flexibility in American universities allowed me to study at my own pace, and as a result, my grades improved. I graduated from UW–Whitewater in December 1971.

The University of Wisconsin system then presented another opportunity to me. The Madison campus had an MBA program that accepted new graduates with bachelor's degrees. Some people prefer to work a few years and then pursue a master's degree. My preference was to finish my academic studies and then focus on working. So I enrolled in the UW–Madison MBA program, and because I had an undergraduate degree in business, it was possible for me to complete the MBA program in about a year. It took me two semesters and a summer school to finish all the requirements. I earned my MBA degree with an emphasis in accounting in December 1972.

By then, I was so sick of studying that I didn't even bother to wait for the commencement ceremony. I got on a plane and flew home to San Francisco and started my working life.

While studying at the University of Wisconsin, I did explore a few extracurricular activities that I found enjoyable. For a short time, I played violin in a school orchestra. Although I had difficulty reading the music sheets on sight, I learned how an orchestra functions and developed a deeper appreciation of orchestral music. I also took a karate class from a Korean instructor. The main benefit I got out of it was good exercise and strengthened muscles. I also took up sailing on Lake Mendota, a beautiful lake right next to campus in Madison. I learned to maneuver a sailboat quite well and enjoyed being outdoors with the sun and wind.

Stephen Chan joined me at the UW–Madison School of Business after he graduated from the Whitewater campus. Another high school buddy, Ed Lai, also attended UW–Madison. His field of study was industrial engineering.

CHALLENGES IN MY SOCIAL LIFE

Under the weight of the physical and emotional burdens of the birth defects, my learning process for pretty much everything took longer than other people. Just like the process of developing reading skills, learning to interact with people took longer too. Because of my restricted vision, I had difficulty catching facial expressions and body gestures, especially under dim light. Quite often during conversations, I would miss jokes and had no idea what people around me were laughing about. Because I couldn't participate in most sports and games, I frequently found myself short of conversation topics. That was another challenge in social situations.

One of my biggest challenges in growing up was learning how to have an intimate relationship with a woman. To begin with, I did not have a sister and the secondary school I attended was an all-boys school. There were girls in the extended family among my cousins, but we got together only occasionally. I did not have the chance to socialize with women until I entered the Hong Kong Baptist College. I participated in some of the events offered by the Catholic Society and later became an officer of that student group.

Although I enjoyed organizing and participating in group activities, I did not start dating women when I was in that school. Basically, I had a self-confidence issue at that time. I didn't know how to explain my birth defects to someone I wanted to be intimate with. I was afraid that I would be rejected. When I was at the University of Wisconsin, I had a few dates, but I never developed a romantic relationship with someone. Intimacy was something I wanted to experience because I was a romantic person. I envied those guys who had girlfriends. It looked like such a wonderful thing. For a long time, intimacy was to me a dream that seemed so distant.

Many years later, I did find the love of my life. I was very fortunate, despite my struggles, to have a love story that I can now share in this book. In fact, one of the noblest love stories I have come to know is my own.

STABILIZING FACTORS DURING MY TEENAGE AND COLLEGE YEARS

Looking back on this period, I consider it worthwhile to summarize the factors that prevented me from sinking into chronic depression, schizophrenia, or some kind of destructive path, despite all the stress I was subjected to. The main factors discussed so far were hardworking parents, a broad formal education, interest in music, empathy for other physically challenged people, and a few good friends.

But there is yet another factor—the Jesuit priests who educated me also taught me how to pray. Although I don't think I had a strong faith back then, I found a sense of peace in praying, and it was particularly comforting during times of sadness and despair. Perhaps because of sensitivity to the suffering of other people, I never felt that God singled me out for torture. I have always felt that there is a higher order that is difficult to understand.

What I didn't see in my young years were some lifelong positive effects RP and PKD had on me. They kept me humble and learning because they always presented a need to know more. With this constant quest to know, my process of growing never stopped. In retrospect, the pain and suffering I encountered turned out to be stepping-stones to higher consciousness. It was through this process that fear led to knowledge, weakness became strength, hurt produced motivation, sadness led to joy, failure turned to success, and rejection became acceptance. Looking back at these causes and consequences, however, I still consider myself a student today—always learning and growing, a work in progress reaching for the higher consciousness from which no one can ever graduate.

Ultimately, that is what makes this life interesting and worthwhile for me.

5

Becoming an Independent Person: Struggling in the Real World

THE FIRST TEN YEARS OF MY WORK EXPERIENCE

I started my working career in January 1973. Despite my academic training, the real world was a very strange place to me, and I soon found that I was totally unprepared for it. It took me a long time to actually relate textbook knowledge to the workplace, and no doubt my birth defects exacerbated this long process. One of the first obstacles to starting my career was my interpersonal skill set.

Ultimately, I had to learn these skills through practical experience in dealing with people. The challenge facing me at that time was adapting to living with my handicaps on one hand and convincing people of my abilities on the other. The learning was difficult, I would say, for the first ten years of my career. Progress was slow, but I did learn valuable lessons.

I had five jobs during this period, averaging a couple years each. My sixth job was a great career opportunity that was worth twenty-six years of my time. I worked a total of thirty-six years after college and retired in 2009.

ERNST & ERNST

When I was in graduate school at the University of Wisconsin–Madison, I became interested in pursuing the certified public accountant (CPA) professional designation. Working for a CPA firm seemed to be the logical way to begin my career. My first job was a staff auditor position with Ernst & Ernst (now Ernst & Young). It took me a while to relate the accounting practices of clients to what I had learned in the classroom.

Auditing is really a good way to begin a career in accounting. At a fast pace, you have the chance to examine accounting records of different organizations. However, I soon realized that the fast pace was not suitable for me. Audit work is always performed under a tight schedule. This type of work strained my eyes because of my impaired vision. So I usually had difficulty completing the work assignments within the firm's expected time frame.

Communication skills are essential for someone to be a good auditor. My communications skills were a struggle back then. Because I was unfamiliar with terminologies and practices in clients' accounting processes, I often didn't know what to ask for in an audit situation. I was also weak in making casual conversations with both the audit team and the clients' personnel. Their social conversation topics were usually football, movies, and cars, about which I knew little. I found it difficult to carry on an interesting conversation and often felt awkward in social settings.

Finally, a partner sat me down and told me that I was not going to have a future at Ernst. That was the end of my first job. I felt very discouraged. That reaffirmed my fear that people wouldn't look beyond my physical handicaps and give me time to prove myself. On the other hand, I said to myself that that was my very first job after college. I wanted to keep going and see what other opportunities I might run into. Although I wasn't a successful auditor, the experience was valuable.

Auditing work gave me a broad perspective of accounting practices and the internal control issues in various businesses. Also, I passed the CPA exam in November 1974, after three attempts. The CPA exam is known as one of the most difficult professional exams to pass. At the time I sat for it, it was a three-day-long test covering four subjects. The test taker had to pass at least two subjects in order to earn the credit, and the passing grade for each subject was 75 percent. My challenge was that my reading speed would not allow me to finish the tests within the given time. I usually could finish about 85 to 90 percent of a test. In order to get a 75 percent passing grade, I had to have a high degree of accuracy in the parts that I completed.

Despite this disadvantage, I did it! That was a great motivation. In the four subjects, I received three scores of 75 percent and one 79 percent.

CROCKER BANK LEASEPLAN

My second job was a general ledger accountant position with the Crocker Bank Leaseplan. My responsibilities included a wide range of accounting tasks, including making accruals and amortizations to income and expense accounts, reviewing all inputs to the general ledger, preparing monthly financial reports, and analyzing fluctuations in revenues and expenses as well as changes in assets and liabilities. I also prepared tax financial statements and schedules. Basically, it was a desk job that was not as fast-paced as auditing.

I found that this type of work was more suitable for me because I had time to rest my eyes. I also learned that despite my slow reading speed, I could be just as effective as my colleagues as I improved in efficiency. It was during this job that I started to connect textbook knowledge to my work, and I actually recommended some improvements in the accounting process and internal controls that were adopted by the company.

I also observed some rather harsh aspects of the real world. The controller who hired me, Mo, told me later that the managing partner at Ernst & Ernst had not given me a good reference, but Mo had hired me anyway because he wanted to give me a chance. Mo taught me a lot about day-to-day operations in an accounting department and how I should interface with him and other staff.

Shortly after I came on board, Mo departed because of some circumstances I was not a part of. A new controller was sent from the headquarters to take his place. With what Mo had taught me, my relationship with the new controller was fine; but about a year later, the company was sold, and I was laid off.

BERKELEY UNIFIED SCHOOL DISTRICT

The job market was quite good during the seventies. It didn't take too long for me to find another job. My third position was with the Berkeley Unified School District as a senior accountant. This job, however, was not as challenging as the last one. The school district was a stale and underfunded organization, but I did not want to keep looking for something else because I had been laid off from my last position and needed a job quickly. Soon after I started, I noticed significant inefficiencies and wastes in the organization.

Some of the people had been there for a long time and were set in their ways and not changeable. One of my responsibilities was supervision of the accounts payable group with a staff of four. The group processed cash disbursements totaling about $20 million per year. I did make some improvements in procedures and implemented accounting systems for the revolving cash fund and the building fund. These were two sets of books that were not yet automated. It was in this job that I started using my knowledge of computerized data processing.

My knowledge and experience in building automated accounting systems would prove useful throughout my career. However, for the most part, my position at the school district was a repetitive job with limited advancement opportunities. I realized I had to look in the job market again. The experience I gained from the school district helped me launch my next job.

FIREMAN'S FUND

Fireman's Fund, one of the major insurance companies, was developing an in-house accounts-payable system and was looking for a systems analyst to be part of its system design team. I responded to the job ad and was offered the position. At that time, Fireman's Fund's headquarters were in San Francisco, and taking public transportation to work was quite convenient for me.

I worked on a team with two programmers and one systems support staff, and the team reported to the assistant controller, who was the executive in charge of the project. My function as systems analyst was to serve as the link between the users and the computer technicians. Designing accounting systems was the part of accounting work I liked. My job in the system development team was to make sure the end users' needs were incorporated in the design of the system. To serve this function well, I had to understand both accounting and computer programming. I worked on the team for about a year, and we were making good progress.

When the system development was substantially completed, the project took a sudden turn. Some high-level executives in the company decided to suspend the project because they needed the computer programmers to work on another more urgent system development related to claims processing. I could see that in an insurance company, a claims-processing system could be a higher priority that an accounts-payable system.

At that time, the accounts payable group processed about $100 million in payments a year in a totally manual system that was inherently weak in providing checks and balances. With such a manual system, there is a high risk of significant errors being left undetected. I felt very frustrated about the suspension of the accounts-payable system development. The team and I had worked hard for over a year on it and had been making good progress. It was very likely now that our work would go to waste.

I learned another lesson in the real world—there are always a number of conflicting priorities in an organization. Whichever priority comes up on top depends on the points of view of the people in charge.

Since the project for which I had been was suspended, I realized my job could be in jeopardy. Fortunately, I was assigned to another position—expense control analyst in the expense accounting group. It was a unit within the controller's department. Fireman's Fund was a very big company; the controller's department had one hundred employees when I was there. There were about eight people in the expense accounting unit. My new responsibility was responding to inquiries about expenses from various departments in the company.

My prior auditing experience was very helpful. This was an easy job, not as challenging as system development. One might think there should be more opportunities for advancement in a big company. That wasn't always the case. I responded to internal job postings several times, only to learn that they already had someone in mind. And when the expense accounting unit had a supervisor position vacancy, management picked a coworker in the unit. I was passed over.

After a couple years, I decided it was time to look for opportunities outside Fireman's Fund. And this time, I wanted to try a smaller company.

THE MAGIC PAN

I resigned from the Fireman's Fund when I got a job offer from the Magic Pan for a special project accountant position. The Magic Pan was a local restaurant company with about ten restaurants in the Bay Area. My first assignment was to investigate receivables created by credit card sales. I completed the project with improvements in internal controls by changing certain administrative procedures.

A few months after I started, the company was sold to a foreign company. I was given another position—financial analyst. Using a time-sharing computer system, I prepared month-end financial statements, including conversion to foreign currency statements. I also analyzed financial results comparing forecasts and budgets; wrote comments for management, pointing out trends and risks; and made recommendations on corrective actions. I enjoyed analytical work and was becoming good at it.

My work at the Magic Pan lasted less than two years. The new parent company went through a reorganization, and I was laid off.

THE ASSOCIATION OF BAY AREA GOVERNMENTS

Fortunately, it took only a couple weeks for me to find another job in March 1983. My next position with the Association of Bay Area Governments (ABAG) lasted twenty-six years and was the last one in my career. It was at ABAG that my career really took off, and my work turned out to be a truly satisfying experience, both for me and for the community I served. I devote a separate chapter in this book to this twenty-six-year period.

HOW MY BIRTH DEFECTS SHAPED MY CAREER

My disorders definitely affected my career choice. My vision impairment steered me away from the civil engineering and auditing professions. The challenge before me in the early stage of my career was to find a less time-critical type of work in order to reduce strain on my eyes. When I felt tired, I had the additional burden of PKD attacks becoming more likely. I certainly didn't have the foresight or a mentor to guide me in the early years of my career. It was a process of trial and error in the real world.

The experience from my first job at Ernst & Ernst was fundamentally important in broadening my perspective on the operations of different types of businesses, but clearly it let me know that auditing was not suitable for me. My second job, accounting work in the corporate office of Crocker Bank Leaseplan, was busy work with deadlines but not as time-critical as auditing. I had time to rest my eyes and to think. I not only produced good work but also proposed improvements on systems and procedures.

My social skills were still deficient. The combination of RP and PKD made me fearful in social settings. I remember one day shortly after I started at Fireman's Fund, my boss, the assistant controller Bob Sandberg, walked over to my desk, bringing with him another manager whom he wanted me to meet. I stood up to shake hands with the guy, and perhaps I got up too quickly, and that triggered a PKD attack. It was one of the most embarrassing episodes in my memory.

I hated having to explain what PKD was. I didn't even know what it was called at that time. Over the years, I had to explain it so many times to friends and coworkers. People were generally fine with it after they understood that it was a disorder of nerves and muscles (that's the best way I could describe it), and they could continue to do business as usual with me. But still I didn't feel confident about myself, and that was why my social skills were deficient.

Also, my eyesight didn't help. I couldn't see facial expressions clearly, so I frequently missed jokes and felt inadequate in social situations. It took many years for me to learn to overcome part of the difficulty by listening carefully to what people were saying. It took a long time for me to learn that I don't need to participate eloquently in every conversation, and it is okay to engage in only the subjects I am familiar with.

Being able to communicate with people with confidence is crucial for success in any career. This was my main obstacle in the first ten years of my career. I was discharged once, laid off a couple of times, and passed over in promotions. It seemed to me during the early years of my career that I would likely be confined to technical jobs and unsuitable for management positions.

However, learning to cope with my birth defects did lead to certain positive consequences. For example, in doing my work, I learned to be careful, to be thorough, not to take *no* as an answer, and to do things right the first time. Gradually, people who worked with me saw these attributes in me, and later they proved to be the foundation of a great career. With respect to the first ten years, I managed to stand on my own feet and made enough money to support myself. That was a great achievement despite the obstacles I had to overcome.

MY SOCIAL LIFE AS A YOUNG ADULT

My family migrated to San Francisco from Hong Kong in August 1969. I returned to Hong Kong from England that year, came to San Francisco with my parents, and continued my college education at the University of Wisconsin. My older brother, Louis, and younger brother, Steve, were already in college. Louis was studying at the McGill University in Canada and Steve at the University of Wyoming. My youngest brother, Anthony, who was fifteen, settled in San Francisco with my parents.

Shortly thereafter, my father went back to Hong Kong to attend to his construction business. He retired in 1975 and came over to settle with Mom. My mother found an administrative job at the Bank of America, in the Chinatown branch. She worked there for fifteen years and retired in 1985 as the head of the overseas department.

After I graduated from the University of Wisconsin with my MBA in December 1972, I went home and stayed with my mother and Louis who had graduated ahead of me and was working in San Francisco. We had a two-bedroom condominium on Pine Street. It was cramped. Louis and I shared a bedroom. Anthony went to University of California–Berkeley. In 1975, we sold the condo and bought a two-unit building on Balboa Street. We lived in one unit and leased the other to a tenant. The two younger brothers were still in college.

Mother, Louis, and I had full-time jobs. My mother was the one who worked the hardest. After her daytime bank job, she still had to prepare dinner for all of us in the evenings. As a bachelor, I didn't have much of a social life during the seventies. I did take a kung fu class in Chinatown for a short while. My limitation in kung fu was that I was not fast enough. My reflexes were slower than my classmates'.

For a period of two or three years, Louis and I took up a ballroom dancing class at the Ling Nan Alumni Association. Ling Nan was the secondary school in Guangzhou that my father had graduated from. The alumni from this school had a clubhouse in San Francisco where they played mah-jongg and held other social functions. There was a group of young people in the dancing class, mainly children of alumni and their friends. Dancing was quite enjoyable.

However, that was not an activity I could excel in because I had problems seeing in dimly lit dance parties, and I had to be careful of making sudden jerky motions to avoid PKD attacks. Another activity I tried but found to be not suitable for me was downhill skiing. Sitting on a ski lift high above the ground was an acute stress on my nerves and sense of balance. I tried it once and knew that I should not go on a ski lift again.

As a young adult, I liked trying different activities to get a feel for my limitations and find out what worked for me. Music continued to be an interest in my spare time. I had taken violin lessons and went to concerts quite often. I participated mostly in groups and rarely had a date with a woman. I was still afraid of being rejected.

IMPORTANT LESSONS I LEARNED FROM MY PARENTS

My parents were worried about me. They worried about whether I could have a stable career, whether I would be discriminated against and displaced by society, and, last but not least, whether I could find a wife. I knew that from my parents' perspective, they were worried about me because they loved me. At that time, though, I wondered, if that was love, then why did it make me feel small and inadequate? Now, decades later, I understand why I felt that way. This kind of attention from them, even though it came from the best intentions, did not recognize my potential and how it could be developed.

Basically, I felt that their parental love put me in a box—a weak child who needed protection—and assumed that was where I would always belong. That put an extra burden on my self-esteem as I was striving to become an independent adult. Because of my parents' mindset, they could not be the people I went to for sharing setbacks of any kind because that would intensify their worry and I would feel even worse. It took me many years to find that if I didn't like the box I was put into, I could get out of it. I did, by struggling hard against it, and I was fortunate enough to run into someone who helped me (chapter 6).

My father passed away in 1998, at the age of eighty-five. One reason I felt my mother and I never fully connected was that she always carried the "poor Joe" attitude. Even though my life was awesome in many ways, she never seemed to share the level of excitement that I felt. Now I can see that she couldn't let go of her worry because, seemingly, worrying about me was part of her love. My idea of love, on the other hand, includes knowing when to let go and let live. My mother passed away on April 12, 2011. It took many years for me to realize that my mother's attitude toward me had a positive side to it. After all, struggling against it as a young adult, in part, propelled me to where I am today.

I don't mean to put my mother under the spotlight. Over the years, I have come to know so many families with communication issues between parents and children. The generation gap is so common across ethnic groups that I believe I can call it a glitch in humanity. The question for me is, what have I learned from my experience with my parents? More importantly, what kind of parent do I want to be?

I have raised two children—April and Kevin. It seems to me that the struggles I have gone through have enhanced my propensity to learn and change. I am by no means a perfect parent, not even close. Being a good parent calls for a learning process. My children grew up in a very different era than I did, and there were things I struggled with in raising them. By and large, we have come through and become closer.

I always remember the difficulties I experienced with my parents and have been determined not to repeat the same issues with my children. April and Kevin have their own families now, and I am happy with my relationships with them. We are open to talk about anything, and over the years, we have learned a lot together. So far, I have been honored and privileged to be their parent.

FIRST ENCOUNTER WITH ROMANCE—OR WAS IT?

Developing self-confidence was no doubt one of my biggest difficulties as a young adult. It got worse before it got better. In March 1977, I married Carol Wong, but that relationship lasted for less than a year. Carol was a secretary in my father's office in Hong Kong. She came to San Francisco for a vacation in December 1976 and stayed at our house. I had never met her before. We went out and had a good time. Within a couple of weeks, we decided to get married. It was a big mistake.

Up to that point, I had never been close to a woman and was very naive. We bought a house on Sunset Boulevard. A few months after we moved in, she started a pattern of coming home late after work and gave me various reasons for her lateness. Later, I figured out that she was going out with another man. When I confronted her with the affair, she acknowledged it and told me that she was not happy.

On Valentine's Day 1978, she came home late again, but

as she was coming through the door, she held up a Valentine's card she had bought for me and told me that was the reason she was late. About a week later, I came home from work one day and found that she had removed her personal belongings from the house, and I never saw her again. I filed for a divorce.

The fortunate part for me was that the marriage ended quickly, and we didn't have any children. My divorce still hit me hard emotionally, though. I felt dismayed about being cheated. Obviously, I was inexperienced and was taken advantage of. I learned a big lesson. This mistake took the innocence out of me, and I wasn't so green anymore.

In some ways, this painful experience prepared me for the love of my life. I met Liena in 1979, and we got married in 1980. Our marriage was a life-changing experience for me, although it did not last as long as I wanted (chapters 6 and 7).

6

A Turning Point—Liena

HOW WE MET

I was busy working at my desk in the controller's department of Fireman's Fund one day in October 1979 when I saw the supervisor of the accounts payable unit walking a new employee around, introducing her to people. She was in a bright red dress, looking pretty nice. He didn't bring her to the expense accounting unit where I worked.

These two units were part of the controller's department with about one hundred employees. There were new employees every now and then, and so I didn't pay much attention to this new staff member until a couple days later. I noticed she was sitting at a desk about fifteen feet from mine with her back facing me. She began to catch my attention. She was always well dressed, and there was a touch of elegance about her.

So when the coffee cart came around, I walked up to her as she was buying her coffee and said, "Hi, I am Joe."

"I'm Liena," she replied with a smile.

NOT EVERYTHING CAN BE EXPLAINED

After the day we said hello, our friendship developed quickly. Seeing each other every day in the office facilitated it. We chatted during breaks, had lunch in the office cafeteria, took walks together after lunch, and went out after work. Liena was very friendly. With her warm personality, she soon became a popular person in the office.

She was divorced and had a four-year-old daughter, April, who was attending preschool. One of our frequent activities was picking up April from school and having dinner with her. April was a bright and cute little girl. One very special thing about April was that she was so natural with me the first time I met her. We didn't need a warm-up period. When Liena and I picked her up at school, she would come running to me first, and even Liena was surprised. She even competed with her mom for my attention.

When the three of us went out, Liena did the driving. April didn't like to sit in the backseat, so she always sat on my lap in the passenger seat, sharing a seatbelt with me. I enjoyed playing with April. She made me feel like a kid again. We got down on the floor and were very creative in coming up with all kinds of funny games. Liena trusted me with April. I was the one to pick her up from school whenever Liena couldn't. Obviously, one of the reasons my relationship with Liena developed so quickly was that April and I were so compatible. Perhaps it was destiny or God's plan.

Why was this little girl so comfortable with me? I couldn't figure that out at the time. Looking back now, I can see some circumstantial factors in April's childhood. Liena's husband was unfaithful to her, starting when she was pregnant. After April was born, Liena asked her mother in Taiwan to take care of April in order to shield her from a marriage that was breaking up. So April spent her first four years with her grandmother and Liena's siblings. April was closer to her grandmother than to her mom. Although she had a lot of love and attention, there was no fatherly figure in her early years until I came into her life. (Liena's father passed away several years before April was born.) When April turned four, Liena took her back to San Francisco to start attending school.

There was one other factor in my relationship with Liena that I couldn't explain. Liena was not turned off by my birth defects. Right from the beginning, I felt that she had known me all my life. She did not give me sympathy but, rather, supported me with understanding and encouragement. She saw me having PKD attacks, and I was astonished that she was always so calm. One day she said to me, "You are not handicapped—because if you are handicapped, so is everybody else!" I was stunned.

All through my life, I had been taught that my birth defects were handicaps. But immediately, I understood what her statement meant—since no one is really perfect, every human being is handicapped in some ways. Her words had a profound impact on me. It felt like I had been imprisoned in a dark room for years, and suddenly someone had opened the door, releasing a burst of sunlight and fresh air on me. She made me cry.

I never knew a few simple words could be so powerful. I never knew what love really was until she said those words to me that day. Her words changed my life, and I am still living through their effects today. Liena was no doubt an insightful person. I didn't know how she got those insights until close to the end of her life. (That part of the story is in chapter 7.)

As we were becoming very close friends, we both felt that we had something for each other. Liena was very polished in people skills. She was way ahead of me. I was stronger in analytical and planning skills. I was more fluent in English, but she was more fluent in Chinese. We were both divorced and looking for an honest and stable relationship. We felt that our different strengths could complement each other's weaknesses. We explored the idea of getting married and what life would be like as a couple. My self-confidence, however, was not mended overnight.

Taking on the responsibility of a family scared me. Could I maintain a stable career? What if I lost my job? Would I be a good stepfather for April? These were some of the questions that made me hesitate before the big decision. Liena seemed to have more confidence in me than I had in myself. We got married on August 22, 1980.

MY OWN FAMILY

I continued to be amazed by the way Liena helped me with my main weaknesses—my people skills and self-confidence. As a married couple, we had intimate conversations every day. I really enjoyed the openness between the two of us. We told each other anything we encountered at work. I trusted her judgment calls, particularly in dealing with people interactions. She taught me the fine touches in soliciting people's trust and cooperation. I had never had a teacher who knew my weaknesses so thoroughly and whose advice never made me feel inferior.

One day, out of curiosity, I asked her what about me she had told her family. She said, "Everything."

"Everything?" I repeated. "Aren't you concerned they might ask you why you married such a man?"

Her answer to that question blew me away.

"I couldn't wait to tell them all about you," she said, "the way you struggled to stand on your own feet despite what you were given."

She brought tears to my eyes again. All through my upbringing, I had learned to avoid disclosing my birth defects because people might be prejudiced. I felt that my self-image was being thrown out the window completely and replaced with a new one Liena was giving me. I liked this new self-image. It made a lot of sense. I was henceforth on par with everybody else. Most importantly, this new perspective liberated me from the fear of myself, thereby allowing me to explore my full potential.

But I didn't fully understand why this woman had so much faith in me. At that time, I was still struggling to establish myself. I did not have a long track record to show her. Wasn't she putting her happiness and April's at risk?

In any event, we trusted each other with our lives. This was the foundation of our marriage. We both worked very hard to be true to each other by sharing our whole being. At the end of every day, after we finished all activities and April had gone to bed, I loved the way we had our intimate pillow talk in each other's arms. We talked for hours sometimes, especially on Saturday mornings.

After we got married, Liena's mother, Tsai Yuen, came to live with us. I have to say that my mother-in-law was one of the most selfless women I have known. She was born in poverty and did not even complete primary school. She grew up in China during the turbulent time of the Japanese invasion. Despite her background, she was caring and generous, and she always put everybody first and herself last. But she was also a strongminded person with her own principles.

I had no complaint about her staying with us. In fact, we enjoyed spending time together as a family, strolling in the park, shopping, and making dumplings and pot stickers. I miss my mother-in-law's pork buns and sticky rice in bamboo leaves. Because of her help with caring for April and later Kevin, Liena and I actually had more time to do things together, such as going to concerts, which we did quite often. I introduced classical music to Liena, and she enjoyed it too.

In 1981, three of Liena's sisters and her brother migrated from Taiwan and came to stay with us. All of a sudden, our house was full of people. The house was crowded and quite often looked messy. This is a challenge many immigrant families have to deal with. I had been an immigrant too back in 1969. I knew I had to help Liena's family get established in a new country. They were industrious people and managed to save up enough money to buy their own house in 1984.

On December 9, 1982, Liena and I had a baby boy. We named him Kevin. He was an eight-pound, two-ounce, twenty-one-inch beautiful bundle of joy. Kevin was an adorable baby, and everybody loved him. There was one big benefit to having two families in one house at this time. My sisters-in-law were all wonderful nannies. There was a lot for me to learn as a first-time father.

I became proficient in changing diapers, feeding, and washing bottles. But I couldn't cut a baby's hair and fingernails because of my eyesight impairment. I certainly appreciated the help we had in the house. On weekends, one favorite activity for the big family was going to Golden Gate Park, a few blocks from our house. We took a few trips to Yosemite and one trip to the Grand Canyon.

Through the years, we tackled many life challenges. When we got married in 1980, I was working for the Magic Pan. Over the next couple years, the company went through extensive reorganization under new ownership. Liena was a wonderful counselor as I got tangled in the office politics. In March 1983, I took up the finance director position at the Association of Bay Area Governments (ABAG) and held that position until I retired in 2009. This twenty-six-year period in my career was filled with challenges and accomplishments.

In the first couple years at ABAG, I encountered some difficulty in establishing trusting relationships with the management team. Eventually, I made very good progress. Having Liena by my side made a world of difference. I couldn't have done so well without her understanding and support. There are so many stories from my time at ABAG that I am devoting a separate chapter in this book to that period.

The relationship between Liena and I was in fact very mutual. She appreciated my points of view too. Although I had a late start, I was learning diligently to be a good manager at work and a good husband and father at home. I supported Liena through many changes in her career too. She left Fireman's Fund before we got married and had a couple of job changes during our time together. Her last career move was becoming a real estate agent in 1986. With her excellent interpersonal skills, she enjoyed the work and was quite successful in it.

LIENA HAD A DIFFICULT HISTORY TOO

Thinking back about how we met and our different lives before we met, I recognize that we both faced many painful challenges. It seems that what we had gone through before we met somehow prepared us for each other. Liena had experienced a difficult past too. Her father, Chen Chi Han, was a colonel in the National Army. He fought many battles with the Japanese, even engaging in hand-to-hand combat. Liena's mother, Tsai Yuen, was born in poverty and was given away by her parents as a young child to an elderly woman. Tsai Yuen said she had only a faint memory of what her parents looked like, and she didn't know her exact birth date. The elderly woman treated her well and gave her a few years of schooling.

As a teenager, Tsai Yuen went into the city to work (probably Chongqing or nearby). Around that time, war broke out with Japan. Somehow, she met the young army officer Chi Han as he was leading his troops through the town. They got married, and Liena, their first child, was born in Chongqing on April 30, 1945, during the Japanese invasion. In 1948, when the Communist Party took over the mainland, Chi Han and his family followed the Nationalist Kuomintang Party as they withdrew to Taiwan, and that was where Liena grew up.

Liena was bright, athletic, and very popular among her friends. She was the oldest of seven children (five girls and two boys). Her father's military salary was barely enough to support such a big family. The family was financially strapped. Being the oldest child, Liena took on a leading role in helping with housework and caring for the younger siblings. Despite shouldering family responsibilities at a young age, she maintained high grades in school, and her scores were always among the top in her class.

After graduation from secondary school, she attended the National Taiwan Normal University in Taipei. During her college years, she had to work two jobs at the same time to pay for her expenses. But still, she completed the program in four years and graduated with a degree in geography in 1968. She was the pride of the family.

After graduation, she took a teaching job in a secondary school and got engaged to Wang Gunn Shu, a young pilot in the Taiwanese Air Force. Gunn Shu had a warm personality and was an energetic young man. He came to Liena's home often and helped her younger siblings with their homework. He became their hero. A few months before their wedding, a freak tragedy struck. He crashed his plane in a training flight and was killed. The control tower heard him yell out Liena's name right before impact. Those were his last words. It was a devastating blow to Liena.

She told me that she encountered some unusual signs after his death. At his funeral, as his casket was being pushed into the cremator, it suddenly refused to move. It was on rollers and was supposed to require only a gentle push. The funeral director asked the family whether there was someone he was clinging to. They asked Liena to come forward to say a few comforting words. She said over his casket that she would do her best to carry on and asked him to rest in peace. The casket then rolled forward, and the cremation was completed.

A few days after the funeral, when Liena was sitting alone in her home, still stunned by the sudden tragedy, she heard a faint knock on the front door. She said in her mind, *If that is you, please knock three more times.*

Indeed, she heard three slow, soft knocks, and then she smelled the scent of his hair gel circling around her. Liena said she was frightened, and she shivered. With that, the scent withdrew and didn't come back again.

The year thereafter was a very depressing period for Liena. Her father encouraged her to take a trip to the United States and perhaps start a new life there. She came to San Francisco in 1970 and, with the help of some family friends, settled and started working. For the first couple years, she barely made enough money to support herself. She went through a number of jobs, from waitressing to working on an office staff. It was during this time that she received news that her father had gastric cancer.

After a period of treatment that produced little progress, he passed away in 1972. Liena didn't even have enough money to go home for his funeral. She was very distraught. One of her friends, Wilson Chu, came to her assistance. He brought her food because she was so distressed that she didn't even want to cook for herself. They became close friends during the ordeal and got married in 1973. However, it didn't take long for Liena to notice that Wilson was having affairs with other women. The marriage was turning out to be a very unhappy one.

By that time, Liena was pregnant. Shortly after April was born on April 24, 1975, Liena took her baby to her family in Taiwan because she knew her marriage was falling apart. She practically would have to take care of April by herself, and she couldn't afford to put her in day care at that time. Liena returned to San Francisco and tried to salvage her marriage, but they divorced in 1979.

Perhaps influenced by Gunn Shu, one of Liena's brothers, Wei Gi, had become a fighter pilot and was serving with the Taiwanese Air Force, over his father's strong objection. Early in 1979, when it was time for April to start attending school, Liena went to Taiwan to bring April back to San Francisco. While Liena was in Taiwan, another tragedy struck the family.

In a formation flight, Wei Gi's plane collided with another plane from his team. The other plane crashed into his cockpit. He ejected, fell into the ocean, and was never found. He was twenty-eight years old and had been married for only a few months. Because Liena just happened to be home, she was the one to break the news to her mother. It was devastating.

Liena came back to San Francisco with April and enrolled her in a preschool. We met in October of that year when she took a job at Fireman's Fund. The rest of her story was my story too.

WHAT OUR RELATIONSHIP MEANT TO US

Liena and I were very compatible in terms of interests and tastes, and we balanced each other's strengths and weaknesses. We were best friends and partners. Liena's people skills came from being the oldest of seven children and working to support herself at a young age. My analytical and planning skills came from coping with my birth defects. The hardships we had endured before we met made us not only survivors but also empathetic people. There was also the magnetism or chemistry between us that could not be explained, but without that, marriage would not be a happy experience. For a long time, I questioned whether I could establish a loving relationship with a woman, take on the responsibilities of a father, and support a family. These questions have been affirmatively answered.

Life wasn't smooth sailing for us after we met, but we faced it together. The life we gave each other was full of joy and gallantry. We certainly needed all the power love could muster to deal with our next chapter—her cancer and death, life's final and biggest challenge.

There are certain experiences in life that are difficult to fully appreciate until we have gone through them, such as the everlasting nature of love. It is true—at least, in my case—that love did not end with death. I was blessed by the experience with Liena, not just once but forever. The rest of this book is a documentary of the many ways this blessing manifests in me.

7

Life Took Another Turn: Liena's Cancer

BEFORE THE DIAGNOSIS

We had a very good family life. I adjusted to my first-time fatherhood well. Kevin was fairly easy to care for in his first few months. I got used to the midnight feeding routine and had no difficulty falling back to sleep. It was a great joy watching him grow. Kevin was impatient and adventurous when he was a baby. He started to run before he could walk, and he fell head over heels, giving himself many lumps and bruises. Fortunately, we had many good nannies in the house. My in-laws bought their house close by in our neighborhood in 1984, and we went over for lunches and dinners very often.

One of the most wonderful experiences of being married for me was fatherhood. To begin with, it takes a miracle to bring a baby into the world. Then you watch your baby grow and observe so many milestones—the first step, the first word, the first birthday, the first day in school, and other memories that you will never forget. I remember the first day we sent Kevin to preschool. He was three and a half years old. Liena gave me the honor of taking him, and she took a picture of us as we were leaving the house. Kevin was dazed.

He didn't understand why we were sending him to a strange place, and he started to cry. I assured him that we would come to pick him up at the end of the day. It was a traumatic experience for him and, to a certain extent, for us parents too. He cried every day on the way to school for about a week.

One morning, April, who was seven years older, comforted him by saying, "I'll go with you."

"No, I'll go by myself," Kevin replied.

I was a little surprised to see his display of tenacity. He seemed to know that he had to handle the ordeal himself. He adjusted to school well after a couple weeks, and soon, he was learning new things and making friends. For Christmas of that year, Kevin and his classmates presented a singing program at school. I was there with my video camera and recorded the whole thing. It was interesting to see that all the parents in the audience were crazy about the performance.

My eyesight did not present a significant obstacle in raising my kids. It did limit my ability to join them in some of their activities such as catching a ball, playing video games, and any activity that required quick reactions. There were other games I could participate in, such as bowling and cycling. Although I could not be good at them, I could achieve a basic proficiency. My average score in bowling was about 100, and I could ride a bicycle slowly.

From my experience, being a good father doesn't mean having to participate in everything the children engage in. It is more important to be there when they need attention and spend time with them. Kids need to know that they are loved. Being a good parent was a learning experience for me. I learned many lessons from them as they went through different stages of growth, and I hoped my coping with physical limitations would serve as an inspiring example to April and Kevin when they faced obstacles in their lives.

Liena and I were each other's counselor in both career and family matters. I drafted Liena's résumé and helped her transition to a new job three times. Shortly before we got married, she left Fireman's Fund to take up an accountant position at the Cinta Oil Company in San Francisco. That was a career advancement for her. In 1981, the parent company of Cinta decided to move the San Francisco operation to Denver. Since we did not want to relocate and our roots were in the Bay Area, Liena took a new job in November 1981 at the Union Sugar Company, a subsidiary of Consolidated Foods Corporation. She worked in their accounting department until 1986.

The job gradually became too boring for Liena. She had little chance for advancement to management because her college degree was in a nonbusiness major. With my encouragement, she studied for and obtained a real estate license. In the mideighties, the real estate market in San Francisco was very active due to rising home prices. I believed that Liena's interpersonal skills would be her strength in real estate sales. In 1986, she started her real estate business as an associate agent with Merrill Lynch. She specialized in residential properties in our neighborhood. After a couple years, she was doing quite well, was making more money than she had in her last job, and had repeat clients.

Liena was a conscientious person. She did everything to the best of her ability and often put a lot of stress on herself. Selling real estate is a competitive business, and in addition, agents frequently have to deal with unrealistic expectations of buyers and sellers. In retrospect, I wonder whether stress might have played a part in the onset of her cancer. Of course, that is only my speculation. In many cases, cancer can be a silent killer. It can creep up on anyone, despite healthy habits and regular medical examinations.

THE DIAGNOSIS

In 1988, Liena's business continued to grow. She had frequent meetings with clients to show properties and assist them with the intricacies of buying and selling real estate. One day in

November of that year, as she was showing a property, she slipped on a wet floor and twisted her leg a little. She didn't fall down and felt fine for the rest of the afternoon.

That evening, she felt a pain in her hip joint, which continued for a couple days and became more intense. She went for an x-ray, which showed that her bones had thinned. A few more tests were conducted, and they confirmed that she had stage IV breast cancer that had already spread to her bones. Her doctors also informed us that the usual life expectancy at that stage was about two years. The diagnosis hit us like a ton of bricks. It was so sad, so tragic, and so desperate.

We had such a wonderful marriage and two wonderful children and were enjoying sharing everything. Just as we were having the time of our lives together, this diagnosis was like a death sentence.

The first phase of the tragedy was shock. It was hard for us to believe that such a catastrophe could happen to our wonderful family. The next phase of our tragedy was sadness. We held the news to ourselves and didn't tell anyone in the family for a long time. Our intimate pillow talks became teary as we shared how we felt. We cried so many times as we tried to comfort each other. Her embrace and understanding were very comforting to me.

Because the cancer was in her bones, she experienced a considerable amount of pain. Every day, I massaged her, and my touch and spiritual support were helpful to her. In this way, we became closer than ever. But the sadness quickly came back and overwhelmed us. The sadness seemed to resemble waves at the beach: it came on and pulled back and came back again.

The third phase of our tragedy was coming to terms with reality. The initial shock and the sadness that followed were like a storm. As the storm began to calm, the question of what to do about it emerged. The first thing to consider was, of course, her medical treatment. Were we getting the best medical advice? Should we get a second opinion? These were the questions.

The University of California, San Francisco (UCSF) Medical Center was the medical facility approved by our health insurance. It is one of the foremost medical schools and hospitals in the country. We went there for all our medical needs and were happy with all their services. Nevertheless, we did obtain one second opinion, which confirmed the diagnosis. The next pressing issue we needed to deal with was what and when to tell our kids.

At that time, April was thirteen, and Kevin was five. This was the most difficult thing. How do you tell children that their mother has terminal cancer? Looking back, this was one area we did not handle well.

We excluded our children from Liena's cancer treatment process and kept them out of it for as long as possible. We should have consulted with professional family counselors. Liena was treated with radiation and chemotherapy. The main medication she took was Tamoxifen. After a few weeks of treatment, the pain subsided somewhat, and she could walk better, with the help of crutches. As her condition stabilized, we decided to go on a family vacation, just to relax and think about our situation.

A VACATION IN MAUI

In December 1988, we took our two kids to Maui and spent the Christmas and New Year holidays there. We figured that Maui, with its beautiful natural setting and warm climate, would be the best place for Liena. We rented a condo close to a beach. It was a peaceful place with nature's music—the sound of the waves and the smell of the sea. Every day we drove around the island, sightseeing, swimming, cycling down the mountain, and sunbathing at the beaches. A couple of unforgettable things happened in Maui.

One morning, we decided to go down to the beach near where we were staying. It was a calm day. We were wading in the water, and I was holding Kevin in my arms. He had just turned six, and we were having fun playing in the waves. Kevin was excited to see the waves coming one after another. All of a sudden, what appeared to be a small wave in the distance grew to be a huge curling wave way higher than my head. By the time I realized the danger, it was too late to run.

It hit us with such a powerful force that it sent me and Kevin flying and landed us at the bottom of the ocean. I lost my grip on him. The wave kicked up a lot of sand, and it was impossible to see. I made a desperate grab but only touched him. I took another desperate snatch, got his foot, and pulled him up, feet first. I got him in the split second of time right before the huge wave pulled back, which would have dragged Kevin out to deep water. This incident lasted only a few seconds, but it felt like an eternity. That day, Kevin was given a second chance to live, and I was given a second chance to be a good father. I have treasured this blessing every day.

This close call had a long-lasting impact on me. Liena's death was natural and God's call. But had I lost Kevin that day, that clearly would have been my fault, and I can't imagine how I could have lived with such guilt for the rest of my life. God spared me this tragedy, and I am forever grateful. This gift of a second chance, in fact, helped me a lot in dealing with Liena's death because it always reminded me that my fatherly responsibilities must be done well.

Liena and I had many heart-to-heart conversations during that week in Maui, gaining understanding of each other's feelings and looking ahead to the side effects of chemotherapy, the impact on her work schedule, and how to communicate with our children and family. In one of these conversations, she shared with me a very painful story from her past that I didn't know about.

When she was attending the National Taiwan Normal University in Taipei, she was sexually molested by a trusted family friend. She didn't tell anyone about it because of her family's relationship with this person. She was eighteen at that time, and the situation overwhelmed her with shame and fear.

I could see that it was still traumatic to her after all these years; she was in tears as she told me her story. I was sad to hear what had happened to her but at the same time grateful that she had shared it with me. She didn't have to tell me, and I never would have known about it, but everyone has a need to be heard and understood. She trusted me with this very private and painful story, and I was grateful for her trust. I told her that was how I felt.

Thinking about what she told me in Maui twenty years after her death, I feel that I am still learning from it. I have a deeper understanding of rape victims. The pain really lasts a lifetime, and one of the most difficult aspects of it is the fear of telling anyone. That is why many of these crimes are not brought to justice, particularly when they are committed by a caretaker, parent, teacher, or clergy. Everyone who has suffered sexual molestation has a need for counseling and support.

When Liena shared with me this painful period in her past, she was facing death. It seems to me that she didn't want to die without telling me about it. She knew that I would stand by her in every stage of her cancer, but there was also a need to ease the pain of sexual molestation that she had been carrying all those years. She was desperately reaching out for understanding and was counting on finding it in the love between us. True love does not disappoint and can really rise above everything.

I felt fortunate to be the one person in her life who was there for her. I grew as a person from this experience too. I developed a deeper appreciation of the background of her point of view about my birth defects: "You are not handicapped—because if you are handicapped, so is everybody else." I finally realized that this lifechanging insight she had given me early in our relationship that had liberated me from my distorted self-image actually had come from her prior experience with people. Every human being is imperfect; and the flaws in people can be physical, mental, or spiritual. She was absolutely right.

LIFE WITH CANCER

When we returned home, Liena continued with her radiation and chemotherapy. The side effects were very noticeable. Her hair thinned to the point that she had to wear a wig. Her weight went up and down, but for about a year, her cancer appeared to have stabilized a bit. Slowly, new lesions began to appear in other parts of her skeleton. Her oncologists changed her medications many times because each drug had an effective period. There is also a limited amount of radiation a body can take—too much will kill the patient. When it comes to treating terminal cancer, doctors just try the best they can with the treatments available, and the outcome varies with each patient. In Liena's case, the treatments appeared, at best, to slow the progression of her cancer for two to three years. But nothing the doctors prescribed could stop it from slowly creeping up on her.

We also tried alternative medicine. Someone recommended a Chinese herbalist in San Francisco by the name of Jin Zhen who specialized in treating cancer. For the last two years of her life, Liena was under Dr. Jin Zhen's care, in addition to her chemotherapy. We didn't want to give up Western medication, but Liena's oncologists did not object to using Chinese herbs to supplement Western medication since there were no sure treatments anyway.

Herbal treatments required a lot of work on our part. Liena went to Dr. Jin Zhen's clinic twice a week. Each time she brought back a big bag of dried herbs that needed to be boiled in a huge pot we bought just for cooking her herbal medication. Each dose of medicine was cooked from a pot full of water down to a soup bowl of thick, black, stinky, very bitter broth. It was torture for Liena to drink it. I was the one who prepared it for her every day. When you are desperate, you try everything.

In 1991, a relative gave Liena a book titled *Recalled by Life* by Anthony J. Sattilaro, MD. The author, a Philadelphia physician, recounted how he had recovered from what had been diagnosed as terminal cancer in 1978 by following a strict vegetarian diet known as the macrobiotic diet. (Apparently, this diet did hold his cancer in remission for a number of years. But eventually the cancer recurred, and Dr. Sattilaro died in 1999.)

The macrobiotic diet was started in America by a Japanese man called Michio Kushi. The diet includes various whole grains, vegetables, beans, and soups, with no meat or poultry. It focuses on balancing yin and yang foods. When this delicate holistic balance of foods is practiced, believers claim that it holds the key to good health and cure for many diseases, including cancer. Michio Kushi started the Kushi Institute in Becket, Massachusetts, to promote this diet and offer conferences, consultations, and cooking classes. The macrobiotic diet is one of the well-known vegetarian diets and has been followed by people around the world. There are macrobiotic food stores and restaurants in the Bay Area, and some of them offer cooking classes.

Liena learned how to prepare macrobiotic food. She and I started this diet, but our children ate regular food. Some of the dishes were quite tasty. I couldn't go on this diet completely because I found that I did need some meats to keep an adequate energy level. After practicing this diet for a few months without noticeable effect on her cancer, Liena felt that maybe she wasn't doing everything perfectly with respect to the diet. Because we were running out of options, we felt that it might be worthwhile to have a personal consultation with Michio Kushi and learn from the master himself. So in the early part of 1992, Liena and I took a trip to Becket, Massachusetts, and stayed there for four days to learn more about macrobiotics.

The Kushi Institute was housed in a rather large building with many rooms for classes and conferences. During our visit, we met people from all over the country and one couple from Canada. We had a private consultation with Michio Kushi. He made specific recommendations for adjusting Liena's diet and cooking techniques. I had a consultation with him as well. I figured I might as well find out whether he had recommendations for improving my eyesight. Michio Kushi said the macrobiotic diet could cure my eye problem too. The one particular recommendation from him that stayed in my memory was that I should not eat chicken because chickens have poor eyesight. I thought I would follow his intuition for a while, and it would not take too long to learn whether it had any merit.

After we got home from Becket, Liena adjusted her diet according to Michio Kushi's instructions, and I too became more diligent in adhering to the master's diet recommendations. At the same time, Liena was still taking her chemotherapy and alternative herbal medications. A few more months passed, and Liena's progress wasn't good. She was getting weaker, the pain was increasing in intensity, and she had problems sleeping at night. For the several years since her diagnosis, I had hoped that one of these various treatments would drive the cancer to remission or slow it down, but increasingly, it seemed like a lost cause. I kept that feeling to myself.

For the sake of the children, Liena wanted to fight to the bitter end, and of course, I would support her all the way. We hadn't gotten the children involved in her treatment, thinking that Liena could hang on for a few more years and they would be older. How do you tell young children that their mother is dying? We honestly didn't know how to do it at that time and weren't prepared. As I said before, this was one part of the process we didn't handle well. In retrospect, we should have sought professional counseling. Above all, children need to be assured that they will be loved and cared for no matter what happens.

With proper guidance, children can survive crisis and grief well. Because we kept our children away from the desperate situation with their mom, the impact on them was drastic when they did learn about it. April found out about her mom's condition when she accidentally came across a medical report

Liena had inadvertently left on her dresser. April was angry, sad, and very worried. The realization put tremendous stress on her. She was in her senior year of high school and was in the process of applying to universities.

As Liena's condition continued to worsen in the second half of 1992, she and I felt it was time to let Kevin know. He was nine years old, and we didn't really know how to tell him. Liena left it up to me. His tenth birthday came in December that year. I went with him to a sporting goods store and bought him his first bicycle as a birthday gift. I then sat down with him in a coffee shop and told him that his mom was very sick with cancer. The first question he asked was "Is she going to die?"

I said, "That is possible. Everybody dies, but we just don't know when. Mom's doctors are doing the best they can for her." I didn't know whether these were the right things to say, but that was what I could come up with. I share more about how Liena's death affected April and Kevin in the next chapter.

The sadness and despair I felt at that time was overwhelming. Many times, I felt I would rather trade places with Liena. It would be easier if I were the one who had cancer. She could take care of me better than I could take care of her. Sometimes I felt like dying together with her. But the incident with Kevin at the beach in Maui had seemed like a mandate from heaven that I could go only so far with my grief; I had been given a second chance to be a good father to these two children. I began to realize that to fulfill this responsibility, I had to find a way to be emotionally detached from Liena's fate as I stood by her to the end. Fortunately for me, the people at my workplace were the most supportive colleagues.

I found that work could be good therapy. The office became sort of my sanctuary. I went there to relax and to indulge in doing things where I could make a difference. In a way, work helped give me a sense of relief from the situation of Liena's progressing cancer. Liena, too, was active in her real estate business, except in her final year. In fact, she did quite well in the three previous years, closing increasing number of transactions each year.

Her last six months were torturous. Cancer in the bone is very painful. She went in and out of the hospital a few times. Increasingly, she had problems bathing and sleeping. I wished I could bear some of the pain for her. In some ways, my caring for her, talking to her, and just being there beside her seemed to bring us closer than ever. She understood my pain too and did what she could to comfort me. She wasn't afraid of dying; what she was most concerned about was how April, Kevin, and I would carry on after she was gone.

A few weeks before she passed away, she said this to me: "You have been a great husband, father, and stepfather; a great manager, staff, and person." It was the most comprehensive recognition I had ever received, and it came from the person who knew me the most. That was my proudest performance review, and it also gave me a set of values to uphold going forward.

THE WAY WE SAID GOODBYE

In January 1993, her condition took a drastic downturn. She began having difficulty breathing because of fluid accumulating in her lungs. She went into the intensive care unit of the UCSF Medical Center on January 18. The doctors inserted a chest tube to drain her fluid. The tube had to go through an incision in her chest for as long as she needed it. That was like torture, and they had to give her morphine continuously. That could not be a long-term solution, but the cancer had spread to her lungs and kept producing fluid in her chest cavity.

Her doctors suggested a procedure to close up the space between her lungs and chest cavity by injecting medication into it. It was not a cure, but the objective was to force the fluid to go elsewhere so that she could breathe better. The doctors told me privately that they were running out of options to offer. They said they would observe her for a couple more days before performing this procedure.

On Wednesday, January 27, I went to see Liena after work, as I did every day when she was in the hospital. As I walked into her room, it was about six o'clock in the evening. Her doctor was getting ready to perform the procedure to seal the chest cavity and was explaining to her that they needed to keep her awake during the procedure. He told us the procedure would hurt, but they would administer morphine to her as she asked for it.

Liena said to me, "I am sorry that you have to see me suffer again."

"Honey," I said, "with what I have gone through, I am good enough for this. You go ahead, and I'll be here holding your hand. Please squeeze my hand if you need more morphine." That was our last conversation.

The tube holding the medication was about two inches in diameter and a foot long. The doctor squeezed the liquid into Liena through a needle as I stood by her side, holding her hand. Almost immediately, Liena had a convulsive reaction.

"Do you need more morphine?" I asked. She responded by squeezing my hand.

Her doctor gave her more morphine. But the convulsion intensified. She opened her eyes wide and didn't respond to me anymore. A few more doctors rushed in with some other equipment. At that point, they asked me to leave the room and wait outside.

After about ten minutes, they came out and said to me, "We are sorry. She is gone. In honor of her wish, we did not resuscitate. You can go in to see her now."

Liena looked peaceful. All the tubes and medical equipment were gone. It didn't look like she had gone through a violent struggle a few minutes earlier. She didn't even look sick. In fact, she looked pretty, like Sleeping Beauty. I kissed her. She was still warm. I said to her, "Don't worry about me, honey. I will carry on. Rest in peace."

At that moment, I was numb; grief had not struck me yet.

I was surprisingly calm. Strangely, I felt a sense of relief. I was alone in the room with her. It was good for me to spend some quiet time with her and gather my thoughts. My first thought was that her suffering was done. She would not feel any more pain, and I was relieved from seeing her suffer.

Then I thought of our final conversation minutes earlier. She wasn't afraid of the pain the procedure would give her but was thinking only of what I was going through. She was so selfless. I thought of our marriage vow—"To have and to hold, for better or worse, for richer or poorer, in sickness and in health, to love and to cherish, 'til death do us part." Our last conversation captured this pledge and fulfilled it. We remained true to each other, to the very last minute.

FACING THE AFTERMATH

The nurses in the intensive care unit who had cared for Liena came in one by one to give me their condolences. They all said how wonderful a person Liena was. One of them said Liena had told her how grateful she was for the relationship with me and the family life she had dreamed about.

Another nurse came in and said to me, "Are you going to ask the family to come over?"

I suddenly realized that I had a lot of things to take care of. The first phone call I made was to my house. April and Kevin were home. They screamed and cried as they heard the news. I told them to get ready because I was going to ask someone to bring them to the hospital. Then I called my siblings and Liena's siblings. Within twenty minutes, they all came. Liena's mother was so grief-stricken that she had to be transported in a wheelchair. She was crying her heart out as she was pushed into the room.

I tried to comfort her by saying, "Look, Liena is in peace now."

"But I am not," she said as she kept crying.

I wanted to do the best I could to comfort everyone. I didn't cry until after the funeral when I was home.

In the week following, I was very busy planning Liena's funeral. There was a lot to organize, working with the mortuary and cemetery and finalizing the funeral ceremony.

Following Liena's will, her body was cremated and her ashes placed at the Mountain View Cemetery in Oakland. One of the reasons we selected that cemetery was that it is accessible by public transportation. That would make it easier for me to visit her grave. Her funeral took place on Friday, February 5. Liena's mother was overwhelmed with sorrow and was attended to by Liena's sisters. It must be very difficult to lose a child. She had lost a son in 1979 in a plane crash and now a daughter. I could only imagine how she felt. My feelings were still numb during the funeral. I was the organizer, and my focus was on ensuring the event proceeded as planned.

I held in my emotions until I was home after the funeral and realized that our home wouldn't be the same without her. I closed the bedroom door and cried. It was my turn to grieve.

In the days thereafter, now relieved of the burden of attending to a dying wife, I turned my focus to April and Kevin. I wanted to help them get back to their schoolwork and other activities. Fortunately, both Liena's family and my family were close by, and they were all very caring. About a week after the funeral, when we came home after a dinner with Liena's mom and family, Kevin said, "I miss Mom." Then he took Liena's picture in his hand and cried. That was the saddest scene after Liena passed away—a ten-year-old crying his heart out as he looked at his mom's picture.

I held Kevin and said to him, "Yes, we all miss her." I wanted to assure him that he still had me and I would be there for him.

April was seventeen when Liena passed away. The trauma impacted the kids differently. I certainly was not prepared to be a single parent and had a lot to learn. A few weeks after Liena's passing, April asked, "Why is life so mysterious, Dad?"

This was how I answered her: "Although I don't have a straight answer to this question, we may have some sense of an answer if we ask the question from a different angle. What if God or the highest authority in the universe explained to us all about life so that everything was known? What kind of creatures would we be if there was nothing more to imagine, to explore, if we could not experience the joy of new knowledge? So, you see, perhaps there is a purpose in the mysteries of life. I think the state of nature is fine the way it is. I wouldn't change a thing."

April's question was a profound one. That is what many religions and schools of philosophy are striving to address. At that time, I wasn't affiliated with any organized religion. I did believe in a creator God but had not dwelled too deeply on spiritual matters (and did not until I was in my fifties). I wondered where God was in all of these events I had experienced. It was much later in my life that I realized that even if we don't have God in mind, God always has us in His. (I discuss my spiritual journey in the last few chapters of this book.)

Liena lived forty-seven years; and thirteen of those years were shared with me, April, and Kevin. Did we have a worthwhile time? Absolutely. That doesn't mean that we did everything well. There were things we would have done differently, but overall, it was a life-changing experience. I have learned so much from our relationship. I wish we could have had more time, but the memories are so precious.

One of the most important lessons I have learned from Liena's passing is that our relationship did not end with her death. In fact, it has continued to grow with me, as I evolve as a person and spirit. It may sound unreal, but this is what I am experiencing. Spiritually, she is still with me in many expanded ways. For example, I am living the rest of my time in her honor and to her tribute and would not do anything that she would disapprove of or that might let her down. Liena and I knew each other so well, and we were so close that I can feel what she would have said to me in any situation. This must be true—if she still exists in some way that is intelligent, she must be thinking of me just as much as I do of her. It must be reciprocal.

In the years that have gone by, I have not really felt lonely because whenever I am by myself, I feel her presence. I've heard many people say love is indestructible. From my own experience, this saying is really true.

8

A Very Difficult Decade

After Liena passed away, the funeral was done, the children went back to school, and I went back to work, I thought my biggest hurdles were behind me, and the road ahead would be easier. It did not turn out as expected.

The subsequent ten years presented some challenges for which I had not prepared. Although all worked out well at the end, it was a very difficult period of time. Many times I wondered why I had so many problems—more than my fair share, it seemed. Ultimately, I realized that I have learned a lot from the process of trial and error and am grateful for all the lessons. I would say one of the most important realizations of this period was that every human life is unique. The three of us—April, Kevin and I—went through very different experiences.

This ten-year period was particularly special to each of us individually and as a family.

APRIL'S PATH

Liena's passing in January 1993 seemed to affect April and Kevin differently. April graduated from high school later that year. Throughout her high school years, Liena and I had not paid enough attention to April partly because we were overwhelmed by the progress of Liena's cancer. April had always been an academic achiever since primary school. Her grades were at the top of her class every year. She was a self-starter and did pretty much everything on her own, including applying for college during her senior year in high school. The Swarthmore College, a well-known private liberal arts college in Pennsylvania, was April's top choice.

Initially, April and I had a disagreement over her college choice. At that time, I favored public universities over private colleges because the latter were twice as expensive. My preference was for April to attend the University of California, but April insisted that Swarthmore College was a better school for her major field of study—art history. I finally gave in because I felt that Liena would have let her go to the college of her choice. So the plan I worked out with April was that since I had enough money to pay for only three years at Swarthmore, she would have to do some part-time work and obtain some grants to subsidize the costs.

What I did not realize was that April had certain unresolved emotional issues that had started back in her early childhood. Although she had received tender, loving care from Liena's mother during her first four years, deep down, she felt a sense of abandonment; and she had never developed a close relationship with Liena. April was closer to Liena's mother, Tsai Yuen, who passed away in November 1994 in San Francisco.

Her mother's death exacerbated April's emotional issues, which gradually intensified and became a full-blown depression during her college years. April's depression was diagnosed to be associated with a chemical imbalance for which she had to take medication. Despite her emotional issues, she managed to get through the first year of study at Swarthmore. Through an exchange program, she got an opportunity to do her second year at the Oxford University in England. Some signs of trouble began to appear in her first semester at Oxford. Her depression intensified to the point that she couldn't concentrate on her work, and many of her papers were late or unfinished. She couldn't continue at Oxford and came home in early 1995.

She stayed home for a short time and then went back to Swarthmore. She started undergoing psychotherapy. Her professors and dean were very concerned, and despite being allowed extra time, she still couldn't deliver some of her work. One good thing about a small liberal arts college is that students get a lot of personal attention.

During 1995, April was seeing therapists both at Swarthmore and in San Francisco when she came home during breaks. She was having drastic mood swings and sometimes lashed out at people during emotional downswings. She also lashed out at herself. On some occasions, she poured a whole bottle of sleeping pills in her mouth but did not swallow them. Sometimes she cut herself with a razor blade and smashed glasses and plates in the house. She called the ambulance on two occasions because she felt that she was on the verge of killing herself.

After Liena's death, I thought I could settle down and focus on raising our two children. I certainly did not have the slightest idea what I was going to face. One of the most difficult aspects for family members dealing with a mentally depressed person is that a layperson usually does not recognize the lashing out as a symptom of emotional disorder and simply reacts to it with anger and frustration. Mental depression is a serious sickness, and it is not just a bad day. A person with mental depression usually needs extended professional counseling and medication as well. I did learn a lot about depression from therapists and psychiatrists.

April struggled hard at Swarthmore, but soon, it became clear that her depression was too much of an obstacle in her studies. She took a leave of absence from the school and came home in summer 1996 and continued with therapy. She still had frequent emotional swings for the following few years. Depression is a big challenge for families in the sense that it is a day-to-day frustration and anguish. As a precautionary measure at home, I put all the sharp knives and alcohol away.

One very strange event happened in 1998. April and I had an argument over my buying her a car. I was concerned about the safety issue because she was sometimes suicidal. I told April that getting a car could be a goal to strive for when she could hold down a job and save up some money. She got angry and said something to me that I didn't want to remember. Even though I understood that her reaction came from her emotional disorder, it was still very upsetting.

As I was preparing for bed that night, I wondered how I would be able to sleep. As soon as I got myself into the bed and closed my eyes, I saw my mother-in-law. It was a vivid sight. Her face looked bright, and she was smiling at me. But she did not say a word. As I was gazing at her, my whole body instantly felt very warm and comfortable. I slept very well that night.

When I woke up, the sun was shining through the window. It must have been about eight o'clock in the morning. Suddenly, I heard April coming up the stairs. That was very unusual because she usually slept until noon. She knocked, opened my bedroom door, and apologized to me for what she had said the night before.

What I experienced that night was a vision and not a dream because with the conflicting feelings in my mind as I was going to bed, I couldn't have fallen asleep that quickly. Liena's mother was one of the kindest and most selfless persons I have known. April was closest to her grandmother. Perhaps she realized the situation April and I were in and wanted to help us. That was an unforgettable experience to me, and it seemed to be a turning point.

April started seeing a psychiatrist, Dr. Linda Garfield, in fall 1997. She was the most instrumental professional in April's recovery process. I too learned a lot from Dr. Garfield about the best things for me to do in my position. Another significant support on April's path was her husband Joseph Goodman. We call him Joey. April met him the second day after she arrived at Swarthmore College, but they did not become close friends and start dating until Joey graduated from Swarthmore and took a job in San Francisco in 1998.

Joey understood April's emotional challenges and was very patient with her mood swings. He came over to our house very often and gradually became part of the family. Joey was good with the kids. Kevin and all the cousins liked to play with him because he was their cheerleader. With continued therapy and a supportive environment, April's emotional depression gradually improved over a four-year period between 1998 and 2001. I could see her mood swings becoming less frequent and less intense, and increasingly, she began to think and care for others.

April and Joey got engaged in 2002. Shortly thereafter, they moved to Atlanta, Georgia, following Joey's job change. They got married on May 17, 2003, at the Faculty Club, University of California–Berkeley. Their wedding was attended by the extended family and many relatives and friends. Everybody had a great time.

One clear sign of April's recovery from mental depression came when she started to care about how other people felt. That seemed to be noticeable in 2000. Gradually, she cared not only about me and Kevin but also about uncles, aunts, and cousins. The younger cousins began to confide in April with their problems. I was very happy to see that change. That made all the anguish and sleepless nights worthwhile. April and I became closer, and we could talk for hours sometimes, about anything that came to mind. In the years that followed, she and I became very trusting friends.

In 2004, April and Joey moved to Chicago when Joey took a job at the headquarters of Sears, Roebuck & Co. April felt that it was time for her to go back to college and finish her education in arts. She enrolled in the Art Institute of Chicago, and with Joey's encouragement and support, she graduated in 2007. Kevin and I went to the commencement ceremony, and it surely was an accomplishment to celebrate after what she had gone through.

April started a small art studio, and she also helped Joey with his side business in publishing game books. April and Joey are really a good match. It is obvious that they have a lot of fun and a lot of love for each other.

They didn't like the cold winters in Chicago, and in 2009, Joey found a job in sunny San Diego at Petco. It was quite a big move from Chicago to San Diego, but they were lucky enough to find and buy a beautiful house. For the next two years, the family spent the Thanksgiving holiday in San Diego with April and Joey. In mid-2011, April told me that they were expecting a baby in January. I was overjoyed and looking forward to welcome their first baby, my first grandchild, and the next generation of our family.

Haven was born on February 1, 2012. Joey got a job at Apple Inc. in Cupertino and bought a house in San Jose, and they relocated in March 2012. Since then, they have gotten together often with me and the extended family. Haven is a very cute baby, and everyone loves to see him.

KEVIN'S PATH

Kevin was only ten when Liena passed away. He didn't immediately know what death was. It took a couple weeks for him to fully realize that he would never see his mom again. I believe the concept of *never* sank in for him after Liena's funeral. He got very sad. I gave him all my attention. Sometimes, he came over to sleep with me. I suggested to the kids that all three of us deserved a good vacation.

In June 1993, I took April and Kevin on a Caribbean cruise. We went aboard the *Holiday*, one of the Carnival ships, for a seven-day trip to Cozumel, Grand Cayman, and Ocho Rios. It was our first cruise. We all had a great time. I wanted to give my children the sense of a new beginning.

April went to Swarthmore College that year, and it was just Kevin and me at home. Fortunately, my extended family was close by. My brother, Louis, lived on the same street; and his two children, Karen and Oliver, and my Kevin went to the same school. My mother had already retired from her bank job at that time and was glad to help by picking up the three kids after school and taking them to her house.

These three kids were together every day and got along really well. Kevin was the youngest. Karen was three years older than Kevin, and Oliver was older by ten months. I usually went to pick up Kevin from my mom's house after work, and very often we had dinner there before we went home. That was pretty much the arrangement until Kevin graduated from high school in 2000 and went on to UC Berkeley. Karen also attended UC Berkeley, and Oliver attended UC Davis. Liena's mother and siblings lived nearby too and were also a big help. The families got together frequently on the weekends.

In the summer of 1994, when Kevin was eleven, I took him to Yellowstone National Park for a vacation. We joined a tour group that went through Utah before getting to Yellowstone. We visited the Salt Lake Temple where the famous Mormon Tabernacle Choir sings. Kevin had little patience for the religious and artistic stuff. He was more interested in the national park. We took a bus ride to Yellowstone. On the way, the view of Mount Teton was really breathtaking. Yellowstone was a different world by itself with its hot springs and wildlife. We had an unforgettable time there.

In 1995, I took Kevin on another father-and-son trip to Washington, DC. Kevin had an interest in American history, and Washington was a fascinating place to him. We visited the National Archives, museums, some of the monuments, the Arlington Cemetery, the White House, the Capitol building, and the Pentagon. There was so much to see in that historical place. Kevin found the space museum especially interesting.

We met up with my cousin Pearl and her husband, T. K. Lau. Both of them worked for the federal government. They invited us to their beautiful home in Virginia. April came to join us from Swarthmore, and we went to the Fourth of July celebration at the National Mall and watched the fireworks. It was quite an experience to be there physically.

We did not go on a long family vacation in 1996. Kevin did not stick to me as much after he turned thirteen. He started high school that year. His high school, St. Ignatius College Preparatory, required its students to do mandatory community service every summer. Kevin's social circle widened during high school. He was quite a popular guy.

Like many parents, I tried to occupy Kevin with a lot of activities after school. I signed Kevin up for piano lessons at the San Francisco Conservatory of Music. Actually, that was the second attempt to stimulate his interest in music. I wanted my kids to develop an interest in classical music by playing an instrument.

Years earlier, Liena and I had bought a piano and had a teacher come to give April and Kevin private lessons. April gave up after a couple years. Her excuse was homework in high school. Kevin showed little patience for practicing. Now that Kevin was a few years older, I thought maybe he could sit down and practice. That effort lasted only a few months. He showed no interest, and I didn't want to force him.

Another activity that didn't last very long was having Kevin learn Chinese. I hired a teacher to give Kevin private lessons at home. He pulled a long face every time the teacher came.

Kevin had an interest in sports. He was on the school bowling team, and he was a football fan. He also liked tennis, soccer, and hockey. On weekends, I went with him to practice bowling at the Japan Town Bowling Alley. Kevin also took riding lessons at Golden Gate Park. Horseback riding is not a sport for me because it requires eye-body coordination. But I liked going to the park with Kevin. I took a Tai Chi class in the park while he had his riding lessons. Kevin was good at playing video games too. He often played interactive games with his friends through the internet. They had a lot of fun with it. I told Kevin that I was fine with it as long as he did it responsibly. He did well in school academically.

Kevin did not give me too much trouble as a teenager. He associated with young people who were decent. He was mischievous to his younger cousins, but they loved playing with Kevin. During his senior year of high school, he told me that he wanted to serve in the military. That was in the year 2000, and the world wasn't peaceful. There were potential conflicts lurking in the Middle East. I made an agreement with Kevin that he would finish his college education first and maybe join the military thereafter. Privately, I was hoping he would change his mind over the next few years.

Kevin attended UC Berkeley and enrolled in the army ROTC program. As time went by, it didn't seem likely that Kevin would change his career preference. Especially after the 9/11 terrorist attacks in 2001, he was determined to serve. I thought long and hard about Kevin's career choice. As his parent, did I want to stop him? Did I know which career was safe? I really didn't know. As his father, what would my best advice be for him?

Finally, I took the position that my best advice for him was that he should follow his passion. We are on earth for a very short time, I told him; whether you live forty or eighty years, it is still a short time in the overall scheme of things. I told Kevin I had always believed that the value of life is not in the length of time lived but in its contents. Because life is so precious, it is important that we follow our convictions and pursue purposes that we find fulfilling so that on the day we die, hopefully, we won't have to wonder what life would have been like had we followed our passion.

There was a very heavy side to what I said to Kevin. In 2003, war broke out with Iraq. Every time I heard in the news that soldiers had been killed, wounded, or captured by the enemy, I felt a chill in my spine. I mourned for them and could only imagine what their families must be going through. Every loss of human life is so tragic.

In his second year at UC Berkeley, Kevin met Marla Ward in the ROTC program. The two of them quickly became close friends. One evening when I was having dinner with Kevin, he said to me, "I am going out with a Caucasian girl, Dad. Do you mind?"

"It is difficult enough to find a soul mate," I answered. "If you restrict yourself to a specific group, you reduce your chances of meeting one. So if you think you have met your soul mate, go for it, because that may be the only opportunity in your lifetime. Even if the relationship doesn't work and it turns out to be a painful experience, you will be far better off than wondering what life would have been like had you followed that opportunity."

Marla was a bright young woman. She had graduated from high school at the age of sixteen and would go on to graduate from Berkeley at twenty. She and Kevin had the same interests, and their friendship developed really fast. They were a good match. Marla, being the oldest one of five children in her family, was calm and organized. Kevin, on the other hand, being the baby of our family, was playful and spontaneous. Marla's sisters and brother loved to play with Kevin.

The next big challenge Kevin presented me came around the time of his twentieth birthday, when he told me that he was planning to marry Marla before his senior year at Berkeley. His rationale was that if he and Marla went into military service as a married couple, they would have a better chance of being assigned to the same military base. My immediate reaction was that getting married at age twenty was way too soon. My strong preference was for him to graduate from college, get a job, save some money, and then get married. Besides, Marla was only nineteen at that time. At their young age, I was concerned that the odds for a lasting marriage were against them.

Of course, I expressed my concerns with Kevin, but it was parental advice against two young people who were in love. I realized I didn't have veto power in the matter. So I suggested to Kevin that he should ask Mr. Ward, David, for his permission to marry his teenage daughter. I didn't have an issue with his girlfriend. It was only about the timing. I was hoping that David would tell them to wait, and I would gladly support him.

Kevin later told me how he had mustered up his courage to arrange a lunch meeting with Mr. Ward at Restaurant Peony in Oakland, a well-known dim sum place that was my favorite. They discussed Kevin's intentions over lunch, and as Kevin told me afterward, Mr. Ward also thought that they were a little too young to get married. But he did recognize that there might be an advantage for the two of them in entering military service as a married couple.

David gave Kevin a few requirements: he had to get his driver's license, finish his college education, and keep his Christian faith. The last two were well underway; Kevin needed to get started on the first requirement. That lunch must have been stressful for Mr. Ward too—months later, he discovered a box of moldy pork buns in the trunk of his car. He had forgotten all about the leftovers from that lunch, Mrs. Ward, Gail, told me.

Kevin worked hard to prepare for his proposal to Marla. He worked many months to save up some money for a diamond ring. I did not pay for it. April helped him find a jewelry store and select a ring, and he bought what he could afford. Reluctant to leave the ring in his dormitory, he placed it in Mr. Ward's custody and asked him to keep it top secret because Marla and her siblings were not supposed to know when Kevin was going to propose. The plan was that he would retrieve the ring from Mr. Ward the day before the proposal.

Finally, on a day in February 2003, Kevin went ahead and proposed to Marla, and she said yes. Marla told me later that I had raised a gentleman; he had gone down on one knee and said the right things. The wedding was set for August that year. They wanted to be married before their senior year at Berkeley so that they could focus on planning their lives together as army officers.

A lesson I learned from bringing up April and Kevin was

that my children take on life missions that are very different from mine. In many ways, I really don't know which paths will lead to good outcomes. Therefore, my role is to be supportive and let them find out what suits them best and learn from their own experience. They always have my blessing in whatever they pursue.

Kevin and Marla got married on August 16, 2003. It was a joyous event attended by both families and many relatives and friends.

Kevin and Marla graduated from UC Berkeley in May 2004 and were immediately commissioned as army officers. They started as second lieutenants. Kevin joined the Armored Division, and Marla got into the Signal Corps. Kevin took on a number of additional trainings such as combat survival, mountain warfare, and air assault. In the spring of 2005, the two of them were assigned to Fort Lewis as their home base. Kevin served in the Armored Division as a Stryker officer. In October of that year, Marla and her unit were deployed to Iraq for a one-year term. Kevin and Marla had their first experience with one of the most difficult aspects of military life—being separated from family for an extended time.

Kevin told me that after he said goodbye to Marla, he went back to their house and felt how empty it was without her. I too learned at that point that when you have someone in your family deployed to a war zone, you are on active duty too, twenty-four hours a day, seven days a week, with no breaks until he or she comes home. I now had a better appreciation of what military families across the nation go through.

Marla completed her tour of duty and came home in September 2006. We had many parties to celebrate that occasion; everyone in the family was eager to hear about her experience in Iraq. Marla was promoted to captain in October 2007.

In October 2006, Kevin changed divisions to serve in the General Staff First Corps at Fort Lewis. In February 2008, he too was promoted to captain. He then joined the Signal Corps and was deployed to Iraq in February 2009. But this time, he and Marla were deployed together.

By this point, almost five years had passed since Kevin joined the military in 2004. Even though I'd had a son serving in the armed forces during these years, the possibility of seeing him go to war was something I hadn't always kept in mind until the deployment date neared. I learned constantly from the news about the number of soldiers getting killed, sustaining disabling injuries, or being captured and executed by the enemy. These news stories sent chills through me. These are realities that every military family has to face.

How do you deal with such stress? People handle it in a number of ways. What helped me was my experience dealing with the progression of Liena's terminal illness. When facing a potentially tragic situation, you have to find a way to detach from the cause of the stress. As Kevin and Marla took off to Iraq, I made an agreement with God. I said to Him, "I am placing these young people in your hands. Bless them so that they will do a good job. Life and death are always your business. I will accept your will. Just reveal your will to me, and I'll trust that you will give me the strength and wisdom to handle whatever is before me."

Spiritually, this was to me a resolution of my fears. If something happened to Kevin, emotionally, I might be devastated; and I knew from day to day I might still worry, but I wanted to make sure that I would be intact spiritually, no matter what happened. I wanted to have this resolution in advance so that in the event I was hit by a storm, I would have an anchor ready. I share more about this paradigm in the later chapters of this book.

Kevin and Marla were assigned to two separate bases in Iraq. They did not stay together. Even though they didn't have to serve on the front line, they had to travel frequently to various stations either in a convoy or by helicopter. It was hard not to worry, considering the number of soldiers killed by roadside bombings.

In October 2009, Kevin and Marla were sent to Camp Taji when both of their units relocated there for certain assignments. They were lucky to be together for the remainder of their deployment. They came home in February 2010. We had a big homecoming party for them. Kevin and Marla took a well-deserved vacation to celebrate Valentine's Day in Jamaica. I was so happy to see the two of them so much in love.

In October 2010, Kevin resigned from the Signal Corps to study for his graduate degree in business at the University of Washington. Marla continued to serve at Fort Lewis. Their military service had changed me somewhat. I frequently watched *The NewsHour with Jim Lehrer* on PBS, and the program occasionally presented an "honor roll" at the end, showing in silence names and photographs of US military personnel killed in Iraq and Afghanistan.

As I saw these faces coming across the screen, I was deeply saddened by their tragic deaths, their being so young and handsome and having their promising futures cut short. I also felt a connection with the grieving families, spiritually sharing some of their pain and sending them comfort and strength. I believe many people across the nation watching this program felt the same way.

I believe it is through this spiritual unity that peace can be generated and hope can still prevail over tragedies. And if the deaths of these young people could bring about an uplift in the collective consciousness of the world, maybe they did not die in vain. This is awareness and sensitivity that I would not have if Kevin and Marla had not served.

A couple months after April told me that she and Joey were expecting their first baby, Kevin told me that he and Marla were expecting theirs. Nathaniel, my second grandson, was born on March 30, 2012. Ironically, these two couples both got married in 2003 and had their first child in 2012. They took very different paths, but having babies is a sacred responsibility for all loving parents. I was and am so happy for them. Kevin and Marla welcomed their second child Betsy on August 28, 2013.

MY PATH AND OUR PATH

The most difficult part of Liena's death to me was her final year. The despair and sadness as the cancer rapidly progressed was overwhelming. The healing process after her death was not as sad, as I found new meaning in the days thereafter. It didn't take long for me to realize that even though she was not with me physically, there was a spiritual connection. It has been almost twenty years since her passing, and not a day has gone by in which I have not thought of her. But the feeling is not sadness; it is more like serenity.

I returned to work the day after her funeral because I believed that was what Liena would have wanted me to do. On my way to the office that morning, I sent this thought to Liena: "Honey, let us walk the rest of this journey together." As I was riding the train across the bay, I also thought of what she said to me a few weeks before she died—that I was a great husband, father, and stepfather and a great manager, staff, and person. As I appreciated her recognition, that also gave me standards to live up to going forward. I wanted to carry on in her honor.

Looking back over all these years, I believe that this set of standards has helped me persevere over the difficult challenges I have encountered. The most valuable lesson I have learned from my losses is that they were merely changes in life. Going through them has deepened my understanding of the truths about life and my empathy for people around me and what they may be going through.

Some members of my family have asked me whether I want to find a wife again. I am always open to that, but I don't feel the need to actively look for one. I am professionally and socially active, and I want to just let it be. After Liena passed away, I met a few women with whom I had friendships and romances that were pleasant experiences. If I never marry again, though, I had the most wonderful marriage, which will continue to enrich me going forward.

My path in the ten years after Liena passed away was very much interwoven with April's and Kevin's. Bringing up the two children presented very different kinds of challenges, and I have learned a great deal from this process. It has been a joy to see them both pursue their own aspirations and become independent and respectable people. I am proud of the paths they have taken.

They both married their soul mates in 2003 and started their own families. That was a milestone year for me too. I had to decide what my future would be from that point forward. Of course, my children and their families are still very much part of my life, but the relationships are different. I have close and very trusting relationships with my adult children. We are now more like close friends. We can discuss anything freely and honestly. I find this kind of relationship most enjoyable.

After I retired in 2009, I had more time to focus on myself, and I established new interests and goals. At age sixty-one, I figured that I would be in the last one-third of my time on earth. The first two-thirds had been good, and I had learned a lot from the journey. I wanted to devote the last one-third to giving back to society and, in doing so, explore further the meaning of my earthly experience.

There are so many issues in society that it is not possible to be involved with all of them. What I can do, I decided, is select a few that are close to my heart and offer direct service and/or financial support. The knowledge and insights I have accumulated on both professional and personal levels are some good tools for me to work with and a foundation to build on.

I devote the rest of this book to two areas. One is my career at the Association of Bay Area Governments, where I worked for twenty-six years, and the other is my evolution as a spiritual being. The physical aspects of life have been challenging for me, but they taught me to think. That process stimulated my interest in the spiritual nature of my existence, and I found that to be very much a challenging journey too.

9

What Makes a Good Career?: My Career at ABAG

I graduated from business school in December 1972 and started working in January 1973. For the following ten years, I worked for several companies, changing jobs every couple of years. It was a process of finding the right company, and it worked the other way too, since I was laid off a couple of times during this period.

The first ten years of my career were difficult in the sense that it took a while to connect textbook knowledge with what was going on in the workplace and to work with the different human dynamics in each organization. Those ten years were not easy for me. I was a slow starter in interpersonal skills, which is an important aspect of establishing a career. Carrying my two birth defects was a burden, of course. It took a long time to learn the skills that would get others to look at my real abilities and trust that I could deliver.

Slowly but surely, the skills started to build up with experience. I became good at designing and implementing automated accounting systems and internal control policies and procedures. In my experience, the keys to success in a career are, broadly speaking, twofold—mastery in a certain field of knowledge and recognition from the beneficiaries of one's work.

Achieving mastery in a subject usually takes a long period of training and practical experience. Being passionate about what one does helps a lot. Passion to me means you like what you are doing so much that you would do it even without compensation. In any profession, the distinguishing factor separating the stars from the mediocre is passion, and those who are passionate about what they do are the ones who are sought after.

Of course, whether one can make a living out of what one does passionately may depend on certain economic and societal factors. The work by some well-known artists, for example, may not be appreciated until after their lifetime. Many spiritual thinkers say that we tend to attract opportunities to serve what we are passionate about. In my career, that seemed to be true.

HOW ABAG AND I CROSSED PATHS AND WHY WE WERE A GOOD MATCH

The Association of Bay Area Governments was formed in 1961 through a joint powers act by the cities and counties in the San Francisco Bay Area as a council of governments (COG) in the State of California. Its initial function was to serve as the metropolitan planning organization (MPO) for the Bay Area region. Currently, there are eighteen such MPOs or COGs in the state. The Bay Area region is made up of nine counties with a shoreline that touches the San Francisco Bay and the 101 cities within the nine counties. Initially, funding for ABAG primarily came from federal and state government sources.

In the association's early years, a traumatic incident happened at ABAG. Because of a weakness in checks and balances while the agency was relatively new, someone in senior management position single-handedly embezzled large sums of agency funds. He carried out the scheme by creating two secret unauthorized bank accounts in the name of the association. Money was intercepted from ABAG's cash receipts and deposited into the unauthorized accounts. Apparently, to avoid detection, the embezzler restored money from time to time plus interest to the legitimate ABAG bank account.

Over a period of two years, from December 1965 through February 1968, the perpetrator deposited a total of $787,923.40 of ABAG funds into the unauthorized bank accounts, and restorations plus interest were sent back to ABAG totaling $326,481.40. When he was caught in February 1968, the net funds embezzled amounted to $461,442.00. His objective in restoring some of the stolen money obviously was to keep the embezzlement under the radar for as long as possible as he used the stolen funds in the unauthorized bank accounts to finance his secret business ventures, probably including gambling. He was convicted and sentenced to jail.

In the fallout from this incident, the state legislature created in 1970 a separate agency, the Metropolitan Transportation Commission (MTC), to manage the transportation funds. ABAG's function was reduced to primarily land-use planning, and it thereby became basically a research agency. So the Bay Area is the only region in the state where the MPO and the COG are two separate agencies. For all other regions, the COG is also the MPO.

This series of events had a tremendous impact on ABAG's operation in terms of limitations in funding and programs. On the other hand, this major setback in ABAG's reputation and function perhaps played a part in enticing creative thinking among the new management team. As a matter of survival, ABAG needed to identify new programs that were beneficial to the Bay Area region and find new funding to pay for them. ABAG started the environmental programs to augment land-use planning in the mid-1970s.

This was a logical program group to embark on since the two subjects obviously impacted each other. During the seventies, several young and talented managers joined ABAG. Among them were Revan Tranter, who became ABAG's executive director in 1973, and shortly thereafter, Eugene

Leong, who was hired to head the environmental programs. Eugene later became the executive director when Revan retired in 1994. The environmental programs ABAG offered gradually expanded to include air quality, water quality, estuary preservation, hazardous waste management, and earthquake preparedness. The agency's number of employees increased to about 120 during the seventies.

A big change happened in 1978 that hit local governments in California like a storm. The voters passed Proposition 13, limiting assessment of property tax to 1 percent of property values and limiting annual increases in assessed property value to the lesser of change in cost of living or 2 percent. One major effect of this proposition was a very significant drop in property tax income for local governments, and consequently, the funding for many government projects dried up.

Over the next several years, ABAG's funding gradually declined, and a number of projects were closed. The total number of employees had declined from 120 to 32 when I came on board in March 1983, and the total agency budget was about $1.5 million for that year. To avoid further staff layoffs, all employees in the agency took a mandatory one day off without pay each month. ABAG was close to bankruptcy.

Concerned about the agency's financial stability, the finance director, my predecessor, resigned for a new job. He was also concerned that ABAG would not be able to repay its office building construction obligation. In partnership with the Metropolitan Transportation Commission and the Bay Area Rapid Transit (BART), ABAG was in the process of constructing a new office building that would house the three agencies.

At that time, I had just been laid off from the Magic Pan due to company reorganization resulting from new ownership. I accepted ABAG's offer, thinking I was still young and could afford to take a gamble with this agency on the verge of bankruptcy. The finance department I was in charge of had only two part-time employees. The accounting system was manual with books of handwritten records.

In retrospect, what ABAG needed back in 1983 was a finance director who could put its financial affairs in good order—and, more importantly, a finance director who would not take no as an answer, who was able to think outside the box, and who was willing to take the risk of growing with the agency. Fortunately for both me and ABAG (and maybe it was a destiny meant to be), I responded to ABAG's open position ad.

My work experience in a variety of organizations in the first ten years of my career served me well at ABAG. My knowledge of accounting system automation and internal control practices was what ABAG needed. Ironically, some of the traumas I experienced in my personal life were actually beneficial in my professional work. For example, in coping with eyesight impairment, I learned to be careful and thorough, to listen well, to plan ahead, and to do things right the first time. These are important attributes in leading a project such as the design and implementation of an accounting system.

The year 1983 was when ABAG's budget and number of employees hit bottom in the downward slide, precipitated by Proposition 13. It seems to me that was the best point in time for me to come on board, redefine systems and procedures from scratch, and prepare the agency for growth from a low point in its history.

SOME NOTABLE PROJECTS AND THEIR DEVELOPMENT

ABAG's success as a regional government agency was the result of the foresight and hard work of many people. I served under the leadership of three executive directors over my tenure and worked with many innovative and talented managers and staff. They were the real champions in establishing new services that were valued by ABAG member jurisdictions and other public agencies.

My role was to make sure every project at ABAG was meeting its stated objectives and was financially sound. That included winding down projects that were unsuccessful (there were only a few in ABAG's history) and doing it in a manner that was legal, ethical, and least damaging to the agency. It is not feasible to list all the successful projects and achievements. Some of these projects were not instantly successful; they went through difficult challenges in their life cycle. The information presented here is from my point of view and recollection and not meant to be a complete history of these projects. Other people at ABAG who worked on these projects may have more information or different points of view. The following is not a complete list, but here are some of the new projects that I worked on closely during my tenure:

THE AGENCY'S FIRST FULLY AUTOMATED ACCOUNTING SYSTEM

When I came on board in 1983, ABAG had a manual accounting system. The first task I took on was system automation. My predecessor had already purchased an off-the-shelf system and was in the process of implementing it.

In reviewing the capabilities of this system, I realized that a number of modifications had to be made before it could serve as the comprehensive accounting system for the agency. My search for a computer programmer didn't take too long because the accounting staff informed me that a high school intern named Atti Williams recently had done some programming work at ABAG. I tracked down this high school kid.

Atti turned out to be a talented computer programmer. With his help, the system was completed in about a year, and ABAG used it until 1999. Atti later became an ABAG employee in the IT department. Through these years, we modified the system many times, serving ABAG's growing needs and also making it run on new operating platforms that became industry standards in the 1980s and 1990s. But this system had two major inherent limitations that could not be changed, despite our purchasing the source codes from the system manufacturer.

The system could not be used after 1999 because of a date issue commonly known as the Y2K bug. The other limitation was that the data field used to identify projects had only two digits, thereby limiting the maximum number of projects to ninety-nine. The significance of this in-house developed system was the length of time it was used, a total of sixteen years, which saved ABAG substantially in information technology costs. It played an important role in keeping overhead costs low during the years of tight budgets.

SAN FRANCISCO ESTUARY PARTNERSHIP

In 1986, ABAG started the Bay Delta Project to conduct scientific research on the condition of the San Francisco Bay with a goal of providing input to develop public policies for preservation of the bay estuary. This project later became the San Francisco Estuary Partnership in the early 1990s. One of the key products of this program is a biennial State of the Estuary Conference where stakeholders examine the ecological health of the bay delta estuary based on the State of the Estuary Report and discuss issues related to freshwater flows, climate change, and management of water resources.

Because the San Francisco Bay is one of the nation's prominent waterways, the estuary program at ABAG receives funding from various federal, state, and local government agencies. The estuary department became the largest department at ABAG. It had about fifteen employees in 2009 and a total budget of several million dollars. The estuary program is a logical addition to the agency because it has been recognized that water resource management and land-use planning are two related fields, and the program provides a dialogue between the two disciplines.

Managing the estuary programs was challenging in a number of ways. Many federal and state agencies that provide funding for environmental projects have restrictions on reimbursement of indirect costs. ABAG's composite agency-wide overhead cost rate usually runs in the range of 40 percent of personnel cost. Many environmental grant contracts limit allocated overhead cost to 5–10 percent of the grant award. The allowable overhead charge under these contracts may or may not be equivalent to ABAG's composite overhead rate.

Budgeting and continued monitoring of these contracts require special management attention to ensure that ABAG's costs are fully recovered. Occasionally, ABAG may undertake a government grant contract that pays below cost. That may be appropriate when a grant requires a local match or when a contract is related to another larger contract.

SAN FRANCISCO BAY TRAIL PROJECT

The San Francisco Bay, together with its inland delta, is one of the largest estuaries in America. Its scale and complexity provide a crucial wildlife habitat, a shipping corridor, and a playground for the shoreline cities. Senate Bill 100, drafted by state senator Bill Lockyer and passed into law in 1987, designated ABAG as the lead agency to develop a plan for the design, construction, and connection of five hundred miles of "ring around the bay" hiking and biking trails.

In 1989, the ABAG executive board adopted the Bay Trail Plan, a set of policies to guide future design, funding, and trail construction. In 1990, the Bay Trail Project nonprofit organization was formed to advocate for grants from government agencies and tax-deductible donations from the general public. I created a separate set of books for this nonprofit to track its operations. Since the passing of Senate Bill 100, ABAG has provided planning and funding for the construction work of connecting more than three hundred miles of trails around the bay. The Bay Trail Project is staffed by several employees at ABAG, and they work with a team of consultants and volunteers.

As the number of projects and affiliated entities under ABAG management grew during the 1980s and 1990s, the limitations of the in-house-developed DOS-based accounting system were becoming increasingly obvious. Changing an accounting system is a big challenge, and of course, we waited until we really had to do it. Eventually, we converted to a new system in 1999.

GENERAL LIABILITY INSURANCE POOL

During the mid-1980s, local governments were facing an insurance crisis. Because of the increasing magnitude of court settlements, insurance premiums in the market surged up so much that many local governments could no longer afford general liability insurance. Responding to this crisis, ABAG introduced a self-insurance general liability pool program for its member governments.

The pool was established as a legally and financially independent entity—the ABAG Pooled Liability Assurance Network (PLAN) Corporation. Its funding comes from actuarially determined assessments to member governments in the pool based on loss history and other factors. We hired a risk manager to head this program who, in turn, hired a team of claim examiners to settle claims against the pool. We started business in June 1986 with twenty-one participating cities and assessed deposits for the first year of about $2.7 million. The pool offered its participating jurisdictions $5 million in general liability coverage. Luck was on our side: the pool did not experience significant claim losses during the first few years, allowing the assets in the pool to grow.

I became the chief financial officer (CFO) of this insurance pool corporation. In addition to financial oversight and reporting, I took on the treasury function, including drafting an investment policy, carrying out day-to-day investment activities, and preparing periodic investment performance reports for the PLAN board. In 2009, the pool had thirty-one members and total assets of more than $50 million, most of which were invested in government agency notes and corporate bonds. It was offering coverage of $10 million per occurrence to its members.

This PLAN program is a valued service to ABAG members. It provides the needed general liability insurance, and because it is a self-insurance program, annual assessments to participating members are far more predictable than premiums of insurance policies in the market, and member jurisdictions also have an ownership interest in the equity of the corporation.

As the program matured, PLAN started offering loss prevention services. Investing in loss prevention proved to be a very effective strategy in reducing claim costs, and risk management through loss prevention programs became a significant benefit for cities participating in PLAN. We offered a variety of programs, including police personnel defensive driving and use of firearms, Stop sign and streetlight installations, sewer system maintenance, and written procedures for disaster recovery.

The PLAN program was a turning point for ABAG. It started the development of service programs. In addition to land-use and environmental planning, ABAG gradually became a multipurpose agency providing an array of fee-for-service programs. The service programs created many new jobs at ABAG and became a significant part of ABAG's total budget. The work was interesting to me as part of the management team, and I developed an interest in investing public funds. Managing the investment portfolio is an important part of an insurance business since the rate of return from investments is one of the key factors in determining premium assessments to cities in the pool.

FINANCING PROGRAM

ABAG started a low-cost and highly efficient credit pooling program in the mid-1980s to consolidate the capital funding needs of participating member jurisdictions. The objective of pooled financing is to achieve issuance cost economy by issuing one bond for a number of agencies in need of capital. These financings were backed by the general fund credits of participating municipalities. Projects financed by this program included construction and renovation of public buildings and purchase and installation of computer systems and other equipment.

In 1990, ABAG established the ABAG Finance Authority for Nonprofit Organizations (FAN), a joint powers agency, to serve as a conduit issuer of tax-exempt bonds for eligible nonprofit organizations to finance projects with demonstrated public benefit. Over the years, projects financed have included hospitals, health care facilities, senior housing, schools, and other community facilities.

By 2009, ABAG had provided more than seven billion dollars in low-cost financings for public-purpose capital projects throughout California. FAN is an independent entity, and the conduit financings it issues are the obligations of the borrowers and not liabilities of FAN or ABAG. The financing program is headed by the financial services manager who has two assistants. The accounting department provides the financial reporting for FAN in a separate set of books.

UTILITY POWER PURCHASING POOL

Energy deregulation in California enabled consumers to buy energy from competing suppliers. In 1997, ABAG began offering an energy aggregation program for Bay Area and other Northern California governments and special districts. The main objective of this program is to achieve the most economical energy costs through the joint purchasing power of participating entities in the pool. An independent joint powers agency was created to operate this program—ABAG Publicly Owned Energy Resources (ABAG POWER). Initially ABAG POWER offered an electricity pool and a natural gas pool, each accounted for as a separate entity in the financial system.

The electricity pool was terminated on July 1, 2001, due to a sudden upsurge in allocated costs from the Independent System Operator (ISO), the organization that manages the power grid in the state of California. The ISO charges were so uncontrollable and unpredictable that pricing of electricity to end users became too volatile and unrealistic. Accordingly, the ABAG POWER board of directors decided that it was prudent to terminate the electricity pool and distribute its assets to member jurisdictions.

The dissolution of the electricity pool was complicated by the bankruptcy proceedings of Pacific Gas and Electric Company (PG&E), the default utility company in Northern California. ABAG POWER was a claimant in this bankruptcy settlement. PG&E owed ABAG POWER $19 million in competitive transition credits. In 2004, the PG&E claim was settled with a payment of $21 million (including interest) to ABAG POWER. With the PG&E settlement, ABAG POWER distributed a total of $24 million to its member jurisdictions in dissolving the electricity pool.

Electricity aggregation was a new experiment in California, and ABAG was the first government group to attempt it. Circumstances were not in our favor, but ABAG POWER continues to look out for an opportunity to reinstate the electricity pool sometime in the future when it is beneficial to its members.

The natural gas aggregation program, on the other hand, continued to operate well. It was not affected by the suspension of the electricity pool. The natural gas pool has two objectives—price stability and cost savings compared with PG&E. The pool enhances price stability by entering into fixed-price contracts with a number of suppliers of natural gas.

These fixed-price contracts specify the delivery of a certain number of units of natural gas within the contract period. ABAG POWER usually enters into several of these fixed-price contracts concurrently, adding up to about 50 percent of the projected total load. The other 50 percent of the load is purchased from the spot market. This strategy is an attempt to balance the risk of market price decline after we enter into a fixed-price contract against the benefit if market prices rise.

In addition to the commodity cost of natural gas, the cost ABAG POWER charges its users include PG&E transportation charges and ABAG POWER administrative costs. ABAG POWER pays PG&E transportation charges for using their pipelines. Therefore, it is a challenge to achieve savings for participants of the natural gas pool in comparison to what they would pay as PG&E customers.

ABAG POWER monitors savings constantly as a measure of its performance. We achieve savings in some years, but not every year, depending significantly on the price of natural gas. By 2009, the natural gas pool had thirty-eight member jurisdictions, and total revenue for fiscal year 2009 was $9 million. Price stability is the primary motivation for participation in ABAG POWER because less volatility in utility costs is important in government entities' budgeting process.

ORACLE FINANCIAL SYSTEM

As the number of programs and affiliated entities at ABAG grew during the 1980s and 1990s, the accounting system developed by Atti and me became increasingly cumbersome because of the inherent limitations described previously. Despite the limitations, we delayed replacing it for as long as possible in order to save money and also because changing accounting systems is just about the worst nightmare for an accounting department. As the year 1999 approached, the alarm got louder and clearer. With its date limitation, I knew our system could not be used after December 31, 1999.

In 1996, I started seriously evaluating the accounting systems in the market and hired a CPA firm to assist in the research. We reviewed demos of the top three systems. Finally, I was convinced that the Oracle Financial System was the one that would fulfill ABAG's current requirements as well as foreseeable future needs.

However, it was the most expensive system; and if we used

it, it would require the IT department at ABAG to upgrade its facilities and have appropriately trained personnel. Personally, I believed that the Oracle option was the best choice over the long term and would prove to be a good investment. When I reviewed our options with ABAG's executive director, Eugene Leong, who was a visionary and savvy in technology, we both agreed that it was time for ABAG to make a big leap forward in computer systems. At that time, there were a couple of other departments at ABAG with expanding databases that would benefit from a robust Oracle platform.

The next thing we had to do was obtain approval from the executive board for an investment in the Oracle Financial System. The board approved an expenditure of up to $350,000 for the project. With this marching order, we signed a contract with Oracle, and after some initial planning, a team of consultants from the Oracle Corporation started a four-month implementation process in February 1998. I had every member of the accounting staff involved in the project so that everyone had some say in the user-defined aspects of the specific models that would become their daily tools.

That added significant extra workload for the staff because they still had to finish their regular work. But this is what it takes to change accounting systems. All my staff had a sense of ownership and commitment in the process, and they rolled up their sleeves and put in the effort.

The reason I started implementing the new accounting system in 1998 was to allow extra time for unexpected obstacles. If something went seriously wrong, we would still have 1999 to finish the implementation before year 2000 rolled around. All of a sudden and out of the blue, the implementation project was derailed by a dramatic event.

On June 10, 1998, three days before the Oracle consultants were scheduled to wrap up the implementation at ABAG and go on to another job, the computer server that held the Oracle system crashed. We checked the backup, and to everyone's dismay, the backup that was supposed to be automated hadn't been working. We had no backup! That meant the work completed by the consultants over the past four months was totally lost. Our original plan had been to go live and start using the system on July 1, 1998, the first day of the next fiscal year. This was obviously a disaster in system implementation and the worst day I'd ever faced at ABAG.

Everybody involved in the project felt very bad. However, we learned many valuable lessons from that experience. First of all, the server had crashed because the small room in which ABAG stored all its computer network hardware did not have a stand-alone air-conditioning system, and so it had overheated during weekends when the office building air-conditioning was turned off. In addition, we had not properly tested the backup system to ensure that it was working. The combination of these factors caused this major setback.

As I calmed down from the shock, I began to think about how to move forward. First of all, I needed to keep the team together. There was a lot of blame to go around for this major snafu, and if I started to point fingers, everyone would duck for cover. After some careful deliberation in my head, I decided my best strategy to get the project going again was first not to indict anybody. So at our regular Monday managers' meeting, I announced the unexpected crash of the Oracle file server and the loss of all the files in it because of hardware overheating and the failure of the backup system.

I went on to say that the Oracle Financial System was an extremely complex system. I was the one who had led the agency onto this path. Although I had expected some challenges and adjustments in using Oracle, I had not anticipated such an event. Nevertheless, this was a learning experience, and we had taken a big step in becoming savvy Oracle users and realizing the benefits the Oracle databases had to offer.

The effects of my little speech were good. Because I had not accused anyone and had taken responsibility for the setback on behalf of the team, people came to me individually to offer their assessment of what had gone wrong and what they thought should be done differently going forward. I believe that I would not have gotten such genuine responses had I ordered them to give me their analysis.

The first thing we decided to do was build a larger computer room with independent air-conditioning. Since the Oracle consultants were all scheduled to go on to other jobs and wouldn't be able to come back until December 1998, we had six months to get the computer room ready and thoroughly test the backup system. The reconstruction of the Oracle Financial System was not as big a job as I had expected. Because the consultants still had the setup documents, redoing the setup was going to be a two-week job by one consultant. The cost of the additional consulting work was estimated to be $70,000.

Just as I was preparing to request executive board authorization of the cost overrun, it came to my attention that loss of computer software was covered by the agency's fire insurance policy, both consultant cost and ABAG staff work attributable to the recovery. Based on my calculation, the total cost for this loss amounted to $90,000. We submitted a claim to the insurance company and received payment in full. That saved us the embarrassment of informing the board about the incident.

In retrospect, "the crash of 1998," as the IT staff called it, was a blessing in disguise. Not only did it cause no financial damage, but it also gave me the opportunity to study the system carefully before the Oracle consultants returned. I came into the office just about every weekend during those six months, sometimes both Saturday and Sunday, to do some of the setup procedures myself. I gained in-depth knowledge about the system in the process, and as a result, I decided to make a number of changes in the system that would better serve ABAG's operation.

We were very fortunate that the system crashed before we went live with it. It would have been a bigger loss, had the system crashed with actual financial data. It seems to me that if the system had to crash in order to let us learn a lesson, it couldn't have crashed at a better time!

After the system was reinstalled in December, I worked on a series of procedures to ensure the process of going live would be smooth and safe. Because ABAG's fiscal year runs from July 1 to June 30, the next go-live date would be July 1, 1999. It is far simpler to begin using a new accounting system on the first day of a fiscal year than to switch during the year (accountants understand this).

Because the current accounting system would drop dead on January 1, 2000, July 1, 1999 was the latest date for ABAG to go live with the Oracle system. That was the goal we had to achieve because there simply would not be enough time before 2000 for us to find another accounting system if the Oracle system failed. We started entering data into the system in July 1999, and the real test of the system would be whether I could close the month of July, the first month-end close, with the Oracle system.

The day of reckoning came on Saturday, August 14, 1999, and I came into the office to perform that procedure myself to see it firsthand. I verified that all transactions had been properly posted, and then I ran the one automated allocation journal entry that was the final step for month-end closing. I clicked the Submit button and watched the Pending indicator flash for what seemed like forever. Finally, it changed to Completed. The system worked!

The feeling was like trying to fly a plane off an island to escape an approaching tsunami. As I turned the ignition, the engine fired up, and the plane took off in the nick of time to slide just barely above the top of a huge tidal wave. That was a feeling of euphoria I'd never forget.

GASB 45 SYMPOSIUM

In July 2004, the Governmental Accounting Standards Board (GASB), the national accounting standards–setting body, instigated GASB Statement 45, requiring state and local governments to disclose in financial reports liabilities related to other postemployment employee benefits (OPEB). The bulk of these liabilities arise primarily from retiree health and long-term care benefits. The objective of this new accounting provision was to disclose the liabilities of the promises to provide these benefits after termination of employment. The need for this regulation was precipitated by the rapid rise in health care costs in recent years.

GASB 45 brought under the spotlight a dilemma this country is facing. At the time these promises were made decades ago, the costs of these benefits were insignificant, but now they have become unsustainable for many government entities. Governments basically are facing two options: (1) start funding OPEB liabilities or (2) scale back these benefits going forward. Option 1 is difficult under tight budgets exacerbated by the sluggish economy. Option 2 is challenged by labor unions.

In a chat I had with Henry Gardner, ABAG executive director, he expressed interest in offering a seminar to assist member jurisdictions in dealing with the OPEB challenge. It took about six months for me to finalize the topics to be presented, line up the speakers, and get other logistics in place. The symposium was held on August 18, 2006. Topics of the seminar included a summary of the requirements of GASB 45, actuarial assumptions and examples based on actual studies for municipalities, funding options and implications, a recent labor negotiation on OPEB costs by one transit agency, impact of GASB 45 on debt issuance, and an investment option for OPEB trust funds. The speakers were all well-known professionals in the respective subjects. The symposium was attended by about one hundred people, and the reviews by attendees were very positive.

Evaluating the comments by attendees of the symposium made it clear that ABAG should offer a follow-up conference. The focus of the first one had been the provisions of GASB 45 and how to comply with them. We needed a second symposium to share actual experiences of various government agencies in implementing the requirements of GASB 45. I spent another six months getting the second symposium ready.

The main topics of the conference were organized in three panel discussions. The first panel discussed the policies and politics of OPEB. The second panel focused on human resource management and financial issues in controlling OPEB costs. The third panel examined bond rating issues related to unfunded liabilities and legal issues related to OPEB management. The panelists included elected local government officials, management and legal staff, and speakers from related businesses. Henry Gardner and I jointly worked on forming the agenda and lining up the speakers. Henry is a well-known figure in the government arena and has broad connections.

The symposium was offered on August 24, 2007. The auditorium was filled to capacity, and again, reviews from attendees were very positive. Clearly, controlling and funding OPEB costs was a challenge facing local government agencies and will continue to be for a long time. In fact, the rapidly growing costs of various entitlement programs are presenting a major challenge for the entire nation; among them, health care costs will continue to be a significant part of the federal government budget, and controlling these rising costs plays a critical role in reducing the federal government deficit.

A RETIREMENT PLAN ASSET MANAGEMENT PROGRAM FOR CALIFORNIA

For retirement plan asset management—401(a) and 457(b) plans—local governments and other public agencies typically engage insurance companies or other financial institutions for investment advice and plan operation services. The dilemma in this industry is that large plans, in terms of total assets, usually get better services and pay lower fees than small plans. The small government entities are disadvantaged by their lack of bargaining power.

In 2001, ABAG, the City of San Carlos, and a number of other government agencies in Northern California started the California Public Agencies Self-Directed Tax-Advantaged Retirement System (STARS) program. By establishing a single trust, agencies would benefit from the collective purchasing power as a group, and all participants in STARS would get the same services and pay the same fees.

We organized a steering committee comprising representatives from the initial sponsoring agencies, engaged the American International Group (AIG) to serve as service provider, and rolled out the STARS program in 2001. I served on the steering committee as the representative from ABAG. Many government entities bought into the STARS mission, and the program grew steadily for several years. At its high point, right before the economic downturn in 2008, STARS had twenty-nine participating agencies and $60 million in total assets. It was around that time that some differences in points of view between the steering committee and AIG became obstacles to the STARS program.

The first sign that we noted was AIG's reluctance to market the program to small entities. Then as the stock market fell during 2008 and 2009, some smaller-member jurisdictions in STARS received letters from AIG notifying them that AIG intended not to renew their contracts under the terms established by the STARS program and they had the option to renew under new terms with AIG. In response, the steering committee terminated AIG's relationship with STARS as of September 1, 2009. Member jurisdictions of the STARS program had to decide individually whether to renew their contracts with AIG or change service provider. This would mean the end of the STARS program.

The feeling among members of the steering committee was that it was a good effort for a good cause, even if we hadn't fully achieved the stated goals. To me, personally, the downturn of the stock market over 2008 and 2009 was like a low tide at a beach, revealing the rocks that had been there all the time. Apparently,

AIG had never really bought into the goals of the STARS program from the very beginning, and they had been treating each member entity in the program as a separate contract instead of as part of the total pool. One important lesson for us, the organizers of the STARS program, was that the setup documents of the program had left open a possibility for AIG to interpret their relationship in the way they did. If the STARS program were to continue, we decided, the plan documents and the contract with the next service provider would be written differently.

In early 2009, by coincidence, my successor at ABAG Herbert Pike and I came in contact with another retirement plan service provider, the Unified Trust Company (UTC). We had a number of meetings with UTC representatives who showed enthusiastic interest in the STARS concept and were willing to work with us to reestablish the program. They gave us invaluable advice on defining the contracts and plan documents and were willing to offer the STARS program a set of competitive fees that would decline as total assets increased. We decided to start the STARS program all over again. The previous members would have to rejoin because the plan documents were different. We also stated the goals of the new program as follows:

Membership—all public agencies in the state of California, regardless of size, are eligible to join, and they will pay the same fees. Total transparency of fees charged by service providers.

Discretionary fiduciary—sponsoring agencies designate Unified Trust Company to be the discretionary fiduciary.

Revenue sharing—revenue distributions from mutual funds to service provider will be passed on to participants.

Governance—sponsoring agencies have the option to appoint a representative to the STARS Board of Trustees.

There were no retirement plan programs in the market that offered all these features. We believed such a program deserved great success because it ultimately would enhance the participants' security in retirement. Most of the previous member agencies decided either to stay with AIG or to contract with other service providers. The STARS program would have to prove itself again.

We believe that the program will gradually become increasingly competitive as more agencies join and assets grow. We organized a new board of trustees, which had its first meeting on September 1, 2009, to approve the new plan documents. Richard Averett, the CEO of Regional Government Services, was elected chair; Herbert Pike, vice chair; and I, secretary. The STARS program was one of the organizations I wanted to support with my time and energy after retirement. (I had retired from ABAG on June 30, 2009.) Richard Averett and I have been working on it since its inception back in 2001. This program is a great public service, and I want to do my part to make it successful. Our vision is to make the new STARS program the standard defined contribution plan for local governments and other public agencies in the state of California. With all the features built into the program, we believe it has such potential.

THE ABAG TEAM

The success of every project at ABAG relied on good teamwork. ABAG had many innovative and talented managers and staff. As shown in the foregoing pages, the programs at ABAG are very diverse. The ABAG organization structure is very flat, with a high degree of autonomy at the program director level. My role was to provide each program with the fiscal management tools needed for an effective operation.

I served under three executive directors during my tenure—Revan Tranter, Eugene Leong, and Henry Gardner. All of them were visionaries and dedicated to the ABAG mission. Last but not least, the growth of ABAG programs during my tenure was also attributable to a supportive executive board.

I really appreciated the support from my colleagues at ABAG during Liena's illness. Over those several years, the office was my sanctuary. As I mentioned before, I went there to relax and to focus on doing things where I could make a difference in order to balance myself when the situation at home was one that I could not change. After Liena passed away, the people at ABAG hired an artist to put an artistic touch on one wall in my office with shades of color and a special texture. It looked beautiful. They couldn't have given me anything better at that time. Art represents life.

MY PROUDEST ACHIEVEMENT

When I started at ABAG in 1983, the agency's budget was $1.5 million. In fiscal year 2009, ABAG's budget was $26.7 million, plus another $22.8 million in the combined budgets of the other affiliated entities. These numbers reflected many changes during that twenty-six-year period. Although this may be an impressive record, the achievement that was most significant to me was recovery of the public trust that had been lost after the embezzlement in 1968.

As we have seen in major scandals in public and private sectors, the fallout from these incidents often triggers corrective regulations that can be overblown and may not resolve the real underlying issue. Instead of focusing on strengthening the internal controls at ABAG, the state legislature of California removed the transportation projects from ABAG and put them under a new agency, the Metropolitan Transportation Commission. From my point of view, the divided management of land-use and transportation planning by two separate agencies for the Bay Area is inefficient and less cost-effective. But ABAG has recovered from the loss of public trust and is now entrusted with managing tens of millions in public funds. The two-agency structure, we cannot change; but in addition to reestablishing its integrity as a public agency, ABAG has emerged as an innovator and has offered many new services to assist local governments and other public agencies in becoming more efficient, effective, and economical organizations.

There is a parallel between ABAG's history and my personal history in the sense that traumatic events presented opportunities for learning, growth, and innovation. There is no question in my mind that being visually impaired made me a better CFO than I otherwise would have been because a good CFO needs attributes beyond being good with numbers. Fortunately, I came to work in a place with many other leaders who had good insights and tenacity.

Over the years, ABAG encountered a number of crisis situations, and there were setbacks. But we learned from each one, and they were all valuable experiences. With limited resources—and often facing difficult political challenges—ABAG's work gained recognition and respect from local governments and other public agencies. In 2006, ABAG conducted a survey of its member governments to study public opinions about the value of ABAG services and areas where members would like to see more or less focus. One of the areas that received the highest scores from the survey was the fiscal management at ABAG.

It is intriguing to note that some of the lessons I learned from dealing with Liena's illness, her death, and, later, April's emotional depression were useful in my professional work too. These personal experiences helped me develop empathy for people. I became more sensitive to what others might be going through in their personal lives. For a manager, empathy for others is the key to building dedicated and lasting relationships.

Honestly, I couldn't have achieved what I did at ABAG without Liena's spiritual support. It took some time for me to realize the influence she continued to have on me after she passed away. Her encouragement, trust, and hope in me lived on. I felt a strong motivation to realize my full potential so that she would be proud of me. I served sixteen more years at ABAG after her death and realized many rewarding experiences, as described in this chapter.

10

Is There A Real Purpose in Life After All?

This is everyone's question, but not everyone has to ask it. I choose to examine this question for curiosity's sake. This is really a lifelong question, many aspects of which have no easy answers. Another motivating factor is that if human life has meaning after all, I want to be enlightened by it to the fullest extent.

WHERE I HAVE BEEN

At this point, probably two-thirds of my life is behind me, and I am in the last one-third. There is a lot to be said about my first two-thirds, which I covered in the first nine chapters of this book. I have survived, managed, and learned from the many challenges thrown at me. I have gone through good schools, a wonderful marriage, and a rewarding career and have raised two children to be respectable people.

In some ways, life is like an opera. I am one of the principal characters in it, but I am also the audience. This is an intriguing concept. Being in the audience means there is a detachment from what is happening on stage. With this detachment, I am in a position to critique what I am watching. What is very special about this life opera is that I have the ability to influence the opera's outcome going forward as I switch between the role of the principal character and the role of the audience every now and then. The principal character's mission is to please the audience, and he needs constant feedback from me, the observer.

Just like an opera I see in an opera house, this opera continues to have an impact on the audience after it is over. The life opera will end too, the part that is played on this earthly stage; and I, the audience, will move on.

Now having watched about two-thirds of this opera, I am happy with the outcome so far. I have learned from the past that my points of view and the choices I made played an important role in shaping the future. How do I want the rest of this story to transpire and end?

THERE IS A LOT MORE TO COME—IT IS A QUESTION OF WHAT I WANT IT TO BE

What will come next is primarily a question of where I want to place my focus. Obviously, I can't possibly experience everything. I am not interested in everything. Knowing my natural limitations, I want to focus my remaining time and energy on understanding more about the deeper truths of life. Who am I? Why am I here? What happens when I leave here? These are very profound questions and most interesting to me. They are also somewhat scary because the answers are infinite and wide open.

People usually prefer definite and straightforward answers. Since one can go through life without pondering these perplexing mysteries, not everyone wants to bother with tackling them. But I have found satisfaction in the pursuit of knowledge and still have a zest for understanding more. This is the joy of enlightenment. It is perhaps the same kind of curiosity about how far I can go carrying the burden of birth defects. These formidable hurdles have kept me humble and thinking. Humility is the foundation for learning and wisdom.

However, I would not call myself wise, for the path to wisdom never ends. I can only become wiser but never wise enough.

Many religions and schools of philosophy attempt to provide answers to these existential questions. It can be difficult to decide which one to follow since most of them claim superiority. I don't think one needs to study all of them in order to make a choice because there are many values in common among the main disciplines. Of course, we are free not to make a choice at all. I want to approach these questions from the Christian model, not from the position that it is superior to the other disciplines, but because it is the model I am most familiar with.

I am not a spiritual teacher or scholar. I consider myself to be always a student, only trying to learn as much as possible during my time on earth and pursuing the truth wherever it may lead. This book is a documentary of what one human being has gone through. I am still evolving, and therefore, there is no need to defend any of my points of view. I don't intend to convert others to my positions, but I am interested in sharing my insights and knowledge and in listening to other points of view and disciplines. If someone finds my experience useful, that will be great; if not, we all will move on. What works for me might not work for everyone.

This book will also serve as future reference for me as I continue to learn and grow. The first nine chapters focused on the significant events in my life and lessons learned. The last four chapters discuss the deeper meanings of life as I see them. This chapter serves as an introduction, and the following chapters cover specific spiritual challenges and their impacts on me.

ARE THERE UNIVERSAL TRUTHS AND ABSOLUTE TRUTHS?

I believe universal truths can be defined as values that are valid in different times and places. I am not a scholar in this, and it is a crude definition at best. For example, the rights to life, liberty, and happiness can probably be regarded as universal truths. Many scientific discoveries have become universal truths that may bring further discoveries over time.

Until about four hundred years ago, people believed that the sun circled the earth. Now we know it is the opposite. It is remarkable how fast the universal truths about nature are changing. We also know now that the sun in our solar system will not always be there. It is essentially a lump of fuel that will burn itself out eventually, some millions or billions of years in the future. The moon that shines on us at night may not always be there either. We know that it is drifting away from Earth slowly at the rate of a fraction of a centimeter per year.

If we look out farther into the universe, which we now have the capability to do through space telescopes, we see that the entire universe is expanding at an accelerating speed. The universe is tearing itself apart and taking us on a ride, and because we are the passengers on planet Earth, we share the fate of our solar system and the universe. One big universal truth, therefore, is that everything in the universe is on its way to somewhere; nothing is sitting still.

Absolute truths, on the other hand, are truths that are not subject to change. Therefore, nothing within the expanding physical universe fits this definition. Absolute truths to me are the truths outside the space-time-matter world, and they are the source and cause of all the changes we are observing. There is a wide spectrum of positions among human thinkers about the source and cause of the universe—from the universe being created by a God for a reason, to there being no source or cause of the existence of everything. Whichever position one picks along this spectrum of beliefs, it is really the most intriguing challenge of human consciousness and has been ever since humankind became capable of intellectual thinking.

HOW DO I KNOW WHAT I BELIEVE IS TRUE AND NOT JUST MY OWN WILD IMAGINATION?

I have heard some people say it is human imagination that created God. From my point of view, it is the capacity to imagine that distinguishes us from the other species and makes a human being far more than a biological shell. Our imagination has led to many scientific discoveries and artistic achievements. To me, the concept of human imagination creating God has about as much validity as music creating the composer.

One significant outcome of my life experience has been learning to trust my own instinct. I believe that my instinct has steered me to the truths of life. For example, in my early childhood, my parents tried to protect me from the prejudice of people over birth defects. They came from a position of love, the best of intentions. As a little child, I did not understand why that kind of love did not give me peace and joy; instead, I felt fear and hurt. Who taught me to feel that way? Where did those feelings come from? Now I know the answer to these questions.

They came from my instinct—or soul, if you will. Even as a little child, my soul knew who I was, and when I was treated as less than who I was or expected to be someone I was not, that led to fear and hurt. I believe every human being is born with this kind of instinct, by which we feel fear and hurt when we deviate from truth and feel peace and joy when we are in harmony with it.

The joy I am referring to is a long-term and consistent state of mind. It is not the same as temporary pleasures. It is the blissful consciousness that is unshakable even during periods of pain and suffering. I have learned to listen to my own instinct and follow it. So far, it has led me to places far beyond what I thought possible. This is the joy of enlightenment that has been leading me on, as I not only survive the adversities in my life but also expand my vision to learn from the experiences of other people and from the messages provided by our magnificent natural environment.

This enlightenment process has enticed my interest in the most fundamental questions of human life: Who am I? What am I made of? Why am I here? And what happens when I leave here? I want to take these questions as a group because I feel that the answers to them are closely related.

According to Genesis 1:26, humankind was created in God's image. According to this description, each human being is a "God-let"—that is, there is a little bit of God in each of us. This is the spiritual or soul part of each person. My soul knows who I am as a given instinct, which comes from being in union with the highest source of creative wisdom.

Each human being has three parents—our biological parents produce the body, and God unites each one with part of Himself. From this point of view, all human beings in the world are truly brothers and sisters. I consider my body to be far less significant than the other part of me that coexists with God, the part that was never born, that will never get old or sick or die, and that is all loving and always seeking new knowledge and experience.

Therefore, every human being is made of the same earthly materials and the same soul fabric (the God who created the universe and everything in it). Yet each one of us is so unique because what we encounter in life can be very different. We are shaped by the environment, the people we meet, and the type of work we do to make a living. We are distinguished by our knowledge and experiences that produce character and beliefs. Although we are shaped by the earthly factors, we are meant to be free spirits. We can see in human history that when free spirits have been suppressed, lives have become unhappy, families have been broken, and dynasties have crumbled. It is the essence of our spirits to seek liberty and happiness.

The soul part of me includes my consciousness—my feelings and thoughts. The body carries out what the consciousness wants to do. Everyone occupies a consciousness that no one can replace. No one can be me, and I cannot be anyone other than myself. This is where each person is unique. The soul of each person bears the signature of the Creator; and just like my personal signature, no matter how many times I write it, no two signatures of mine are the same. God created me only once in the entire history of the universe. Because I am also part of the highest creative wisdom, I coexist with God outside the space-time-matter world where there is no past or future—there is only now. I was sent into the space-time-matter world for a short time to experience God's various creative purposes. After the biological phase of me is completed, I will return to the now where I always belong.

Another way to look at my body is that it is a vehicle in which my soul resides through this earthly journey. It is the divine intent to give each human being an earthly journey so that we may experience His magnificent creativity and learn about and develop a relationship with Him.

Faith, spirituality, or consciousness has to make sense and be applicable to real life. When faith is based on reasoning, it consistently brings me peace, joy, and fulfillment. Otherwise, I would need to seek a different discipline. My faith has been a source of inspiration and guiding light for what I want to do in the life that is still coming. In the following chapters, I present some of the specific spiritual topics I have struggled with and learned from.

11

Faith: The Truth Sets Me Free

INTRODUCTION

Let me first reiterate that I am not a spiritual teacher or scholar. This chapter summarizes some of the meanings of life I have struggled with and my current views on them. I don't intend to convert others to my points of view. In fact, I don't even claim to be right. My views are what make sense to me, and I am just a person who is always interested in seeking enlightenment. My intention is to pursue the truth, wherever it may lead. Although my views may evolve, that doesn't mean that they are shaky. I have realized that learning is an infinite path and a rewarding one. I want to elaborate further on the thoughts presented in chapter 10, particularly on my difficulties with faith and how it has transpired in me.

WHAT IS FAITH ANYWAY, AND HOW MUCH DO I NEED IT?

Given that we live in a world of incomplete information or knowledge, faith is the belief that something is true or something is false. We need faith to function well in day-to-day living. Faith can be something as intuitive as believing a chair will support my weight before I sit down on it. Another example is that before I deposit my paycheck in a bank account, I need to believe the money will be there when I need it. Without this kind of faith, I would be too busy checking on everything and could accomplish very little. Faith is, therefore, very much experience-based, not only my own experience but the experiences of other people as well. In fact, one of the primary factors in the development of human civilization was our ability to accumulate and communicate knowledge with others.

It is important to note that human imagination, the creative part of our intellect, is a key factor that leads us to new experiences. Everyone is born with the ability to imagine. It is probably true for everyone that there are times when imagination is obstructed by false beliefs. False beliefs can block us from experiencing the full potential of our highest self, or soul. The issue is not whether someone is smart or dumb, but it is a matter of the highest self being active or dormant.

Because faith is experience-based, it can easily be shaken by events that are contrary to one's beliefs. For example, our environment can suddenly change with very short notice—as in a natural disaster, acts of terrorism, or diagnosis of a deadly disease. A trusted person can turn out to be an embezzler or a pedophile. As we build up defense mechanisms to protect ourselves, that may also lead to stereotyping and misperceptions.

In my childhood, I was led to believe that people were biased about birth defects and that I should try to hide them. That was a false belief. Of course, some people are prejudiced, but many are caring and helpful. If I try to hide my difficulties, that only creates more misunderstanding. Over several decades of experiencing, the truth I have learned is that every human being is somewhat imperfect. Therefore, there are no disabled people in the world; everyone is just differently abled.

Going deeper in this truth, I see that God does not make anything defective or anything that is junk. Defectiveness is only a human point of view. Everything happens for a purpose. Someone may ask, "How about the devil?" The devil is no junk because evil ultimately shows what righteousness is. (I have more to say about this point later.) Even my sister, Mary, born with a heart condition that limited her life to nine days, made an impact in the world. She was loved and missed.

I was only four years old at that time, but I vaguely remember how she looked. I remember how my mother cried after she passed away. My parents wanted to have a girl, and they had one for nine days. Perhaps, she was a messenger, and the message she brought was that human life is not meant to be perfect and it is through imperfection that we find knowledge and build character, joy, and hope. Actually, a lot can be said about her short nine-day life.

The human experience includes not only events but also thoughts and intuition. Intuition is in fact an important element of faith. We use our imagination to complete the picture from the tidbits we can observe. But how do we know whether our gut feelings are true? Our gut feelings come from our highest self—that is, our soul, part of the intelligence that started the universe.

Our soul naturally gravitates toward the truth. In my experience, I feel peace and joy when I am in harmony with truth and feel fear and hurt when I deviate from it. This is a guideline I find reliable in forming my own faith system. This is not to say I am self-absorbed and out of touch with others. In fact, it is very important to evaluate different points of view. We do benefit from the knowledge and insights of people from all walks of life, but at the end of the day, I decide what makes sense to me. This is the process through which I grow in my faith; my consciousness shifts as new meanings of life come to light.

The final three chapters of this book are a documentary of the specific spiritual topics I have struggled with and my current position on them. All these beliefs are what I hold to be true as of this writing and are subject to change, since they are profound topics, and I am always on a path of continued education and enlightenment.

IS TRUTH A MATTER OF OPINION?

Although human perception of the truth can be very personal, there are certain truths in the universe that are the same for everyone, regardless of one's knowledge or points of view. Over the ages, some universal truths were discovered as new knowledge came to light. For example, when the Italian scientist Galileo published his observations about the earth orbiting around the sun and other workings of the solar system, these observations came into conflict with the Roman Catholic Church because in their opinion, these teachings were incompatible with the scriptures. In 1615, Galileo was tried and put under house arrest for the rest of his life. In 1992, Pope John Paul II offered an official apology in recognition of the error in Galileo's sentence. It took 377 years for the institution to formally change its opinion. But better late than not at all.

Although some truths are scientific, many others are not. Love is an example, and so is pain. It is difficult to define love, but everyone who has experienced it knows what it is. When I was misled with false beliefs as a little child, I felt pain. From my experience, both love and pain are real and not matters of one's opinion.

IS THERE A GOD?

This has been the biggest question ever since human beings became capable of intellectual thinking. One model of belief holds that there is no need of a God because the universe always existed. It has no beginning or ending. Scientifically, that doesn't seem to be true.

Our space telescopes have observed that all the galaxies in the universe are escaping from a common point—a distant point from which they all came, a point where time began, about 13.7 billion years ago in a huge explosion called the big bang, before there was no time and no space and all matter was in one very dense point. The big bang was not an explosion like a bomb. If it was too weak, everything would have collapsed back together by gravitational pull. If it was too strong, everything would have been blown apart; and galaxies, solar systems, and planets could not have taken form.

From its very beginning, the universe seemed to be facilitating the future development of life. Could all this have happened at random without cause? To me, it makes sense to believe that there is an intelligent source outside the time-space-matter world that caused it to begin, with a plan for everything that happened thereafter. It takes a bigger leap of faith to believe that the universe happened at random without cause. This position is illogical to me.

We know that the past is not infinite. The future does not appear to be infinite either. We also know that the universe is not only expanding but doing so at an accelerating speed, propelled by the "dark energy." This phenomenon seems to suggest that the universe will have an ending. The fact that it is expanding at an accelerating speed might mean that it has passed its midlife. Nothing in the universe is stable; everything is going somewhere—out.

The sun in our solar system is only a lump of fuel that will burn itself out sometime in the future, although it may still have millions or billions of years left. The moon that shines on us at night is drifting away from earth by a fraction of a centimeter each year. With the mirrors left there in previous manned moon explorations, we can now measure the moon's distance from earth accurately by shining a laser beam at it.

Our planet is not stable either. In its approximately 4.5-billion-year history, it has gone through many periods of violent environmental changes, with mass extinctions of its inhabitants. There was also an impact by a huge asteroid colliding with earth about 65 million years ago, which resulted in the extinction of the dinosaurs. Based on the latest archeological findings, human beings have been around for only a few million years. This period of time in which the conditions have been suitable for the human species is only a small window in the lifetime of planet Earth. This window of suitability is subject to change, as it has been in the past.

So what do all these observations mean? They are telling us that the entire universe is temporal, and we are just part of the whole story. Should we feel gloom and doom? The answer hinges on whether there is a purpose to human life and some form of existence when it ends. This series of questions is circling back to the first question—is there a God? This is really the most fundamental question. If it is logical to believe that there is a God and that He had a purpose in creating the universe and everything in it, then it is also logical to believe that God has a purpose for the end of the time-space-matter world.

We don't know for sure what form of existence there is beyond human life until we die. My position on the subject of life after death is to ask two questions: Who am I? And what am I made of? It is clear to me that I am not just my biological body because there is the other part of me that appreciates beauty, is capable of love, and has a natural tendency to gravitate toward joy. This is the part that came from the same source of the universe, or soul, or God—the part that is outside the time-space-matter world that has no beginning or ending. If this is what I am made of, then who am I?

A Bible message is becoming more meaningful to me the more I think about it: "Be still, and know that I am God" (Ps. 46:10). This is a very profound message. In one interpretation, this message can be referring to the Creator God, and we have to be still to feel His presence. It can also be interpreted this way: "Be still, and know that I (Joseph Chan) am God." This interpretation is no exaggeration or blasphemy if the soul part of me comes from God, is a "God-let," and is always in union with God. If God is infinity, part of infinity (me) is infinity.

We studied this concept in mathematics back in high school. A fraction of infinity, no matter how small the fraction, is infinity. This view is true with every human being. If each one of us is God, do we have all the godly qualities? Are we omnipresent, omnipotent, and omniscient?

Our bodies are the part of us that is limited in all three ways. The biblical account of Jesus's resurrection suggests that we will share some of these qualities when we shed our biological shell and return to the existence from which we all came. Just like the resurrected Jesus, we don't need time to travel anywhere; certain things we want done will happen instantly; and we will have a comprehensive point of view after we leave the time-space-matter world.

However, the fact that we have these godly characteristics does not mean we will have all the powers God has. Jesus said, "No servant is greater than his master, nor is a messenger greater than the one who sent him" (John 13:16). In another message, Jesus clarified who we are and our relationship with God: "You are my friends if you do what I command" (John 15:14). A friend to me is a peer, someone with whom one is free to agree or disagree. Jesus elevated us to his level in this statement. What about the *if* condition in this message?

From the standpoint that I am a "God-let," God's commandments are all part of my spiritual nature or my highest self. Following these commands is essential to my well-being and happiness. If I deviate from His commands, I am actually at odds with myself. Jesus, in his teachings, always talked from a position of the highest authority. The question is whether Jesus was the true God as he claimed to be or was only a spiritual guru. My struggle with this question is a long story, which is covered later in this chapter.

The next question is, if the next phase of our existence is so good, why were we all sent here to earth? Why don't we just have the perfect, all-loving, eternal existence? Why create this temporary and chaotic earthly place? I believe God wants to experience the contrast in the many dichotomies—light and darkness, righteousness and evil, joy and sadness, love and hatred. God wants the satisfaction of experiencing the time-space-matter world. Just knowing is not enough; He wants to experience what He knows.

God also wants to share this experience with beings at His level, beings with whom He can have a relationship, and so He created humankind. He wants to experience, through the lives of each one of us, the outcomes of these dichotomies on earth and the consequences of where we stand in between these paradoxical extremes. I experienced in my youth pain and suffering because I didn't yet understand at that time the truth of life, but it is from there that I eventually found the truth. God wants as many of us as possible to experience the positive poles of these dichotomies and how they are ultimately revealed by the negative poles.

I can say that it is true in my life that through pain and suffering I have learned and am still learning about who I am, what I am made of, why I am here, and what happens when I leave here.

HOW DOES EARTH HISTORY RECONCILE WITH THE BIBLE?

To me, the Bible is not a science book, and it is not a step-by-step procedural manual on how God created our world. Even if we believe that the Bible is the word of God, it is not possible for God to tell us all about Himself in a book. I believe that the source of everything is so infinite in complexity that it cannot be fully described in human language.

Some Christians believe that God created the universe in six earth days and the universe is about six thousand years old. Based on the story in Genesis, chapter 1, God created the universe and living things in it over six days and rested on the seventh day. There have been a number of proposed interpretations of Genesis 1 regarding how this story may reconcile with scientific observations. The sequence of events in Genesis 1 contradicts scientific observations in a number of ways.

For example, earth was created on day one and the sun on day four, and vegetation came on the third day, predating the sun. From my point of view, scientific observations do not invalidate the Bible because the Bible is meant to be a metaphorical book, and we probably could never understand some of the deepest mysteries of creation while we are on earth anyway.

I have heard the theories of evolution and creation being debated as if they are opposing positions. My view is that the two concepts are not mutually exclusive. According to the Bible, God created the first human from dust: "Then the Lord God formed a man from the dust of the ground and breathed into his nostrils the breath of life, and the man became a living being" (Gen. 2:7). This description indicates that God created a man using materials He had previously created. If we human beings came from dust, there is a possibility that all living things came from dust, including the animals and vegetation. It is the will of God that makes everything possible.

He created the universe from nothing and continues to create at His timing. Evolution does not prove that there is no God. Rather, it reflects miracles only the Divine Providence could call forth; as indicated in Genesis 2:7, organic material came from inorganic material. If that is the case, cross-species evolution does not violate the Bible. The objection to the concept of apes being the ancestors of humans is somewhat an egoistic issue.

Human beings like to think that we are special, and it is difficult to accept that we are the descendants of animals. According to the latest scientific research, if we trace the evolution tree far back in time, mammals evolved from fishes in the sea, fishes evolved from lumps of cells, and at the beginning of this process, hundreds of millions of years ago, these lumps of cells were a single-cell organism. The evolution process is still continuing; going forward millions of years, some species may become extinct and new ones may emerge.

The belief that the universe is six thousand years old probably comes from the biblical account of Jesus's genealogy. In Luke 3:23–38, from the first human (Adam) to Jesus, there were seventy-six generations: twenty generations from Adam to Abraham and fifty-six generations from Abraham to Jesus. And according to the Bible, the earliest humans lived hundreds of years before they died. So perhaps people estimate that the time span over these seventy-six generations was roughly four thousand years, allowing for longer life span for early humans, plus the two thousand years from Jesus to the present day, which makes six thousand years. I don't support this belief.

In my family history presented in chapter 1, there are 140 generations between me and the first name in the record, and it is correct to say that I am the son of that person who lived about 4,600 years ago. I don't have a complete list of names for every generation in my family tree, particularly the earliest generations. To me, the twenty names from Adam to Abraham in the biblical account were only the known names. According to the best evidence we have, the universe is billions of years old and human beings are the latecomers. We've been around for only several million years.

The important scientific observation is that the past is not infinite. There was a beginning of everything—time, space, and matter. And that is one significant agreement between science and the Bible.

Another potential conflict between nature and the Bible is that if animals appeared on earth hundreds of millions of years before human beings, then death came before sin. I had an opportunity to seek guidance on this issue from Dr. William Lane Craig, professor of philosophy at the Talbot School of Theology. His position is that nothing in the Bible suggests animal death is due to the fall of Adam and Eve (see e-mails between me and Dr. Craig in the later part of this chapter). I agree with his interpretation.

IF GOD IS GOOD, THEN WHY DOES HE MAKE PEOPLE SUFFER?

This is one of the most paradoxical questions. The real question behind this question is this: Is God indifferent, harsh, or evil? My position is that God created everything in the universe. He is the all in all, the alpha and omega, the complete story.

In the complete picture, God created many dichotomies, opposite poles. We need the opposing poles to have contrast; we need to have choices, consequences, and a sense of direction. For example, unless there is darkness, we won't know what light is; unless there is pain, we won't know joy; unless there is hatred, we won't know love; unless we have encountered evil, we won't know righteousness; until we have sinned, we won't know forgiveness and how it feels to be forgiven. In other words, the negative ultimately reveals and amplifies the positive.

Another version of this question is, When good people suffer, how is that fair? We usually hear people asking this question when they are in pain or when they see innocent victims of accidents, crimes, wars, and natural disasters. I certainly asked the "why me?" question in my young years. Absolutely nothing I did caused or made me deserve my birth defects. They brought me tremendous amounts of physical and emotional pain. It was not until many decades later, in my senior years, that I realized the purpose and value of what I had gone through.

I learned that each human being has strengths and weaknesses. The challenge for me is to maximize the potential of my strengths and manage my weaknesses. I learned that from God's point of view—each one of us is special. Therefore, there are actually no "handicapped" people in the world because each one of us is differently abled. What is defective is only a human perspective. During my suffering, I criticized God for being unfair. Now I know my tribulations have led me to certain knowledge, skills, and insights that I otherwise would not have.

Of course, I cannot speak for everyone. What purpose and value do other people see in their pain and suffering?

Ask the parents whose child was abducted and murdered. Ask the person who was paralyzed in a car accident. Ask a survivor who lost everyone in his family in a natural disaster, and so on. Human life can change drastically in an instant, and it is extremely difficult to see any meaning in a situation that is excruciatingly painful.

Over a lifetime, we do see occasional positive consequences of the most painful events. We have seen new laws enacted for finding missing children. Charitable foundations have been established for medical research and disaster relief. Early warning systems have been developed to warn the public of severe weather. Positive consequences may come out of disasters caused by human actions too, such as wars. The atrocities of large-scale violence can change human awareness, although not always. The United Nations was formed after World War II to serve as a forum for resolving conflicts among its member nations; maintaining international peace and security; and promoting social progress, better living standards, and human rights. Some positive aspects of a human catastrophe could be realized over hundreds of years.

HOW MANY GODS ARE THERE?

Many people have criticized the Christian belief in one almighty God as too exclusive. In most ancient mythologies, there are multiple spiritual deities. However, there are a number of observations of nature that suggest everything in the universe comes from one source.

The big bang is a strong piece of evidence that the entire universe came from one mind that sent everything on its way in one powerful action that was beyond human description. We can see the work of this one mind everywhere in the universe, such as in the gravitational pull of matter and in light, heat, water, and all the minerals that are found everywhere in space. Here on earth, there is only one atmosphere that we all breathe, and we all drink the same water. There is only one *you* and one *me*, but we are all connected and part of the whole. From my point of view, everything in the universe seems to be part of a huge oneness.

What does this oneness mean in a practical sense? This oneness worldview helps to raise the level of compassion for people and the environment. Actions by one person, one community, or one country can have far-reaching ripple effects on the world. With the communication media of the modern age, the world in fact has become increasingly close-knit community in many ways. When a natural disaster strikes one region, assistance from all over the world starts pouring in within hours of the incident. Because of availability of information, people of our time have more opportunities to help others, participate in political or social causes, or even pray for people in need.

Spiritual connection can bring a positive impact. Medical studies have shown that prayers do have a positive effect on the ones who are being prayed for. I have a personal interest in helping homeless children. Perhaps the struggles in my own childhood have made me more compassionate with children; seeing them suffer breaks my heart. They are the most helpless. Just in the Bay Area, there are about three thousand homeless children, and there are hundreds of thousands throughout California. Many charitable organizations have been established to serve disadvantaged children locally, statewide, and worldwide.

A CASE FOR JESUS

Most people believe that there is a creator God from whom everything came into being, but not as many people believe that the Jesus of Nazareth in history books and the Bible is God. The story in the Bible about Jesus—who performed miracles, preached about love and forgiveness, was crucified and resurrected, and then ascended into heaven—sounds like a fairy tale to many. Christianity was tarnished throughout history by many atrocities committed in Christ's name. The Crusades during the Middle Ages were among the most egregious examples. These acts of violence were in direct contradiction to Jesus's teachings. Jesus would be appalled by killing in God's name.

Throughout history, Christianity has been used by governments as a means to colonize other countries and to control their people. Christians have been criticized for claiming superiority over all other religions, demonizing other faiths as idol worship, but yet they themselves are hypocritical, falling short of Jesus's teachings of love, forgiveness, and service. In fact, there is little evidence that shows Christians are better parents; perform better in school; or are more honest, kinder, or gentler to strangers than the general population.

Over the centuries, all these issues have turned many people away from Christianity. In my own personal history, I was baptized at an early age because my mother was a Catholic. I attended Catholic schools and studied the Bible as a subject every school year. That was my exposure to the Bible. Every Sunday, my mother brought us children to church. My father didn't find churchgoing to be his thing. My interest in Christianity changed while I was attending the University of Wisconsin. I felt that believing in Jesus was not the exclusive way to be righteous.

There are a number of other religions that believe in a creator God and that have saintly people in their faiths. In my own personal experience, I had prayed to God but not to Jesus during times of trouble, and that seemed to be comforting. So Jesus was not necessary. That was my position for a very long time.

I did not go to any church from age twenty-five to fifty-five. I felt that organized religions were all somewhat biased, each claiming to be the right path and striving to recruit members. I looked down on Christians who went to church every Sunday as simpleminded people who needed to be told that they were okay.

After age fifty, my views began to change. All through my life, I have been challenged with stereotypes, and perhaps that instilled in me an interest in the truth about everything—anything that makes life interesting and meaningful. Looking back at my life, I saw that I had experienced a wonderful marriage, had raised two good children, and had enjoyed a successful career. What else would bring further interest and meaning going forward?

I always have had an interest in various scientific and philosophical disciplines. As I passed through middle age, I developed an increasing interest in the deeper meaning of life. There was one event that seemed to be a catalyst for change.

In 2002, my son, Kevin, invited me to a lecture at UC Berkeley, where he was studying. The speaker was Dr. William Lane Craig, professor of philosophy at the Talbot School of Theology in La Mirada, California. The topic of the lecture was the existence of God. The first thing I noticed when we arrived was that the auditorium was packed. There were hundreds of people in attendance, and some latecomers had to watch the lecture on a TV screen in an adjacent room. I was surprised that this topic could draw such a huge audience in a place such as Berkeley. Dr. Craig's lecture was very inspirational, with his logical approach to the topic. I discovered later that he had a website featuring great resource materials, including his articles, books, lectures, and debates. What appealed to me was his approach to faith with reasoning and not just "the Bible says so."

Over the following couple years, I read some of his publications. One of his books, *Theism, Atheism, and Big Bang Cosmology*, was particularly interesting to me. After reading this book, I sent Dr. Craig an e-mail asking his advice on some questions, though I didn't expect to receive a reply from such a well-known scholar, author, and speaker. This was my initial e-mail:

> Date: Sun, 16 Oct 2005 18:13:02 -0700
> From: Joseph Chan <jklcsf@gmail.com>
> To: jeanettelcraig@yahoo.com
> Subject: Follow-up Questions
>
> Dear Dr. Craig:
>
> I have finished reading your "Theism, Atheism and Big Bang Cosmology" book and found it very intriguing. However, I am still struggling with reconciling the apparent process of creation, the Big Bang and the biblical description of how the universe was created. For example:
>
> If indeed God took billions of years to create the universe as the Big Bang observation suggests, then could the 6-day creation process described in Genesis 1 be interpreted as "6 phases" or "6 days on Gods calendar" and not ours?
>
> If living creatures appear[ed] on planet Earth over hundreds of millions of years, then death must have occurred before sin, and not after sin as a punishment. What is your position on this issue?
>
> I will be extremely grateful to get further guidance from you on these difficult issues. Thanks again for your book.
>
> Sincerely,
> Joseph Chan

To my surprise, just over a week later, he did respond:

> Dear Joseph,
>
> I normally don't carry on discussions via email,

> since I don't even type properly. But let me briefly address your questions in reverse order.
>
> Look again at Gen. 3 and Rom. 5. Nowhere is it suggested that animal death is the result of the fall.
>
> I don't think this is a good solution. I'd prefer some sort of literary solution, e.g., taking the days as metaphors. See Henri Blocher Genesis One for another solution.
>
> Bill

From my point of view, if Genesis, the first book of the Bible is not true, we may as well disregard the rest of the Bible. Since this e-mail exchange, I have studied different interpretations of Genesis 1. My own interpretation of this story of creation is that it is not meant to be a step-by-step explanation of how God created our world. How God actually did it is probably far beyond what our human minds can comprehend. Personally, I prefer the symbolic interpretation of the six days of creation.

Science does not disprove the Bible; rather, it helps us to understand how magnificent God is. The big bang, for example, is one strong piece of evidence in nature that the story in Genesis is true. The time-space-matter world began about 13.7 billion years ago. God is the source of it all, and He has a purpose or many purposes in creation. Of course, there is the opposite atheist point of view that the big bang suggests there is no need for a creator and the universe popped into existence by itself without cause. So we have two choices—either God exists or He does not.

My choice of what to believe is based on the view that something cannot come from nothing, and therefore, there is a God. This is a choice that every human being is free to make. There is no test-tube kind of proof about God's existence. But I believe this is so by design. If there is no room to question God's existence, then there is no need for wisdom and we would be a very different kind of creature.

The significance of this development in me is the realization of the many points of views among Christians. In fact, many Christians are open-minded and reasonable in their faith. Over the past ten years, I have embarked on a journey to explore the question about Jesus. Is the Jesus story in the New Testament of the Bible true? To make a long story short, I will start with my conclusions from this struggle.

The most important event to look at in answering this question, from my point of view, is the resurrection of Jesus. If the resurrection was a hoax—that is, if Jesus did not physically come back to life after death—that would mean the end of Christianity immediately. There are a couple of possibilities under which the resurrection might not have happened. One alternative scenario is that Jesus did not die from the crucifixion. He somehow survived the injuries and woke up. From the description of the injuries he sustained, this does not seem possible. Even if he survived the nails, he couldn't have survived the spear thrust to his side and into his chest cavity.

Another possibility is that his disciples stole his body from the tomb while the guards were asleep, reburied it somewhere, and then proclaimed that Jesus had risen. After Jesus was crucified, all his disciples went into hiding. They were devastated to see that their leader—who had calmed a storm, walked on water, cured the sick, and raised people from the dead—couldn't save himself and were also afraid the same fate would befall them as followers of Jesus. But in a matter of days, they all came out from hiding to proclaim the resurrection, and most of them were martyred. Could so many of them have died for something they knew to be false? People die for the truth, not for a lie. It is reasonable to conclude that they were transformed after seeing the resurrected Christ.

So far, over the last two thousand years, there hasn't been any evidence disproving the resurrection of Jesus. Many books have been written that cast doubt on the Jesus story. Recently, a book by Dan Brown titled *The Da Vinci Code* presented a story in which Mary Magdalene was married to Jesus and their marriage produced descendants. The question such a story raises, though, is that even if it were true that Jesus had a wife, would that make him not who he said he was? My answer to this question is no. Being married to a woman would not diminish what he did.

Here is another observation about the relationship between Jesus and Mary Magdalene: Four people who were close to Jesus stood at the foot of the cross and witnessed his crucifixion—Mary, his mother; his disciple John; Mary, the wife of Clopas and his mother's sister; and Mary Magdalene. As Jesus was hanging on the cross, one thing he did was seek to take care of his mother. He said to his mother, "Woman, this is your son." Then he said to John, "This is your mother" (John 19:25–27). As he was enduring extreme physical pain, Jesus demonstrated he was a good son and a responsible one. Being the responsible person he was, had he been married to Mary Magdalene, he would have made some arrangement for her as well. If Dan Brown's intention for his book was to drum up interest in the personal life of a historical figure and make some money for himself, he was successful. The book sold millions of copies and was turned into a film. If his intention was to shake up the foundation of Christianity, he is barking up the wrong tree.

If the resurrection story is true, that is really the greatest story for humankind. If Jesus physically rose from the dead, then we can confidently believe in all his teachings because by his resurrection, he proved himself to be who he said he was. When one realizes the Jesus story is true, it answers some of the most mysterious question in the universe such as why did God create the universe and humankind and what relationship does He want with us?

Thinking from the big bang to Jesus, it makes sense to believe that the overriding purpose for creation was love. And love is personified and demonstrated by sacrifice and service. Jesus came and taught us what sacrifice and service God offered us through him. Jesus demonstrated to us that God is not an aloof being high up there in heaven; but He is intimately involved with our lives, giving us His understanding, wisdom, and love. God wants to have a loving relationship with us. A loving relationship has to involve at least two parties, and it has to flow freely both ways. The conventional thinking is that we need God, but actually, God needs us too. He wants us to love Him back.

Jesus made this point very clear and explained how to do it:

> Love the Lord your God with all your heart and with all your soul and with all your mind. This is the first and greatest commandment. And the second is like it: Love your neighbor as yourself. All the Law and the Prophets hang on these two commandments. (Matt. 22:37–40)

Loving our neighbor goes hand in hand with loving God. How we treat one another is very important in God's eyes. In Jesus's words, "Truly I tell you, whatever you did for one of the least of these brothers and sisters of mine, you did for me" (Matt. 25:40).

One very essential condition for love to take place is that it must come out of free will. God created the universe out of free will—that is, He did not have to do it. Neither was Jesus forced to come to this world to sacrifice and serve. He did it out of His free will. Likewise, God wants us to love Him back out of our free will. This brings up a contentious issue. Are we really free?

By the way he allowed himself to be arrested, humiliated, and crucified, Jesus demonstrated God's will to do all He could to protect our freedom of faith. When the servants of the chief priests and the elders of the people came to the garden of Gethsemane to arrest Jesus, one of Jesus's disciples drew a sword, striking one of the servants of the high priests and cutting off his ear. We read this event here:

> "Put your sword back in its place," Jesus said to him, "for all who draw the sword will die by the sword. Do you think I cannot call on my Father, and he will at once put at my disposal more than twelve legions of angels? But how then would the Scriptures be fulfilled that say it must happen in this way?" (Matthew 26:52–54)

After he said this, Jesus restored the man's ear. After they crucified Jesus, the chief priests, the elders, and the people hurled insults at him, saying,

> "He saved others, but he can't save himself! He's the king of Israel! Let him come down now from the cross, and we will believe in him. He trusts in God. Let God rescue him now if he wants him, for he said, 'I am the Son of God'" (Matthew 27:41–43).

With a flip of a finger, Jesus could have come down from the cross, flanked by angels with trumpets blasting. The whole world would have worshipped him then, but if he had done that, the people would have had no freedom of faith and thus would have become God's puppets. Jesus's suffering clearly demonstrated that that is not the kind of relationship God wants with us. It is really unfathomable that the creator God of the universe would go to that length to demonstrate His love for humankind. This is really the biggest lesson in humanity—that love must be freely given and freely received; otherwise, it is not love. If Jesus is truly God, then his teachings must be true.

As I am getting older, there is one particular message that I find increasingly real. This particular passage from the Bible is notable:

> As Jesus went along, he saw a man blind from birth. His disciples asked him, "Rabbi, who sinned, this man or his parents, that he was born blind?" Jesus answered, "Neither this man nor his parents sinned, but this happened so that the works of God might be displayed in him" (John 9:1–3).

One major benefit of getting older is the opportunity to look back and observe how one's life has transpired. It is human nature to view disease or bodily defects as punishment. I too have struggled hard with this issue. I did nothing wrong, so why was I given impaired eyesight?

Now, I do see that had I not been visually impaired, my life could have followed a very different path. I might have taken on the civil engineering career path instead of accounting. It is not that one career is better than the other, but I became good at managing money and organizations. Being visually impaired taught me to make the best use of limited resources and helped me develop empathy for other people.

A very different perspective emerged for me—the "why not me?" question. Jesus must have asked, "Why not me?" before he came to this world. He is the only one who could have done what he did. Through his sacrifice and service, he taught us how to ask the "why not me?" question and how to realize our full potential.

Many of Jesus's teachings don't make sense on the surface because they are against conventional thinking and human nature. His teachings "Ask and you shall be given" (Matt. 7:7) and "If you have faith small like a mustard seed, you can move a mountain" (Matt. 17:20), for example, sound out of touch with real life. As a young man, I thought these sayings were naive. Jesus was advising us to think outside the box. His teachings turn human nature upside down. Jesus was a radical. There is nothing conservative about following Jesus.

To reach God's kingdom, his followers were instructed to "forgive others who offended us" (Matt. 6:14), "carry our own cross" (Matt. 16:24), and "be salt and light for the world" (Matt. 5:13–16). If we follow human nature, none of these goals can be accomplished because human nature calls for an eye for an eye, seeking the easy way out, and serving self first. Following human nature is like the flow of water; it only goes downhill. This inherent pull perpetuates some of the root causes of destruction—grudge, greed, and lust.

Jesus has offered hope and help to those who want to follow him. He said, "Come to me, all you who are weary and burdened, and I will give you rest" (Matt. 11:28). Notice he didn't say, "Give me your burden and I will take it away." To win over human nature is like paddling upstream, even with Jesus's help. And he made it clear: "Whoever does not take their cross and follow me is not worthy of me" (Matthew 10:38). To me, he is saying, "If you don't intend to do the human part well, don't count on me helping you" or "God helps those who help themselves." Jesus was not out of touch with real life; he was very straightforward and down-to-earth.

To liberate ourselves from the grip of human nature, we have to recognize the nature of human life. Life in this world is temporal, and some of the things that are pleasing may ultimately cause destruction. Take heed of Jesus's advice: "The man who loves his life will lose it, while the man who hates his life in this world will keep it for eternal life" (John 12:25). Apostle Paul said in Romans 12:2, "Do not conform any longer to the pattern of this world, but be transformed by the renewing of your mind. Then you will be able to test and approve what God's will is—his good, pleasing and perfect will." It is in this godly consciousness that we have the creativity and strength to realize our full potential.

It took me a long time over decades—perhaps I am a slow learner—to understand that the fact that some Christians are hypocritical, are judgmental, or hold other unchristian attitudes does not diminish Jesus's teachings. It only underscores the huge challenge in living up to his standards. Few can really do it consistently; most of us fall short every now and then. I realized in my spiritual journey that there were times when I was misguided by certain ideologies and held false beliefs. I need redemption too.

I have learned that the key to wisdom is humility because that is the condition in which learning can take place and change is possible. If one thinks that he is right all the time and knows a lot, that becomes a stumbling block for learning. In Jesus's words, "The last will be the first and the first will be the last" (Matt. 20:16).

IS JESUS EXCLUSIVE OR IS HE INCLUSIVE?

Perhaps one of the most frequent complaints about Jesus is his claim that he is the only way to the kingdom. "I am the way and the truth and the life. No one comes to the Father except through me," we read in John 14:16. That sounds like a narrow path, doesn't it?

The conventional human thinking is that there are usually many ways of doing things, and so there must be multiple ways of going to God. What about all those people who lived thousands of years before the birth of Jesus and those who have never heard of Jesus even in the modern day? If Jesus is the true God, this statement is timeless and all encompassing.

In John 8:58, Jesus said, "I tell you the truth, before Abraham was born, I am." To some of the people who lived in Jesus's time, these words from a man who kept claiming that he was God sounded like blasphemy. That is why they eventually put him to death to silence him. If Jesus had not physically risen from the dead, at best he would be only one of the many spiritual gurus in human history. It was through his resurrection that Jesus proved to the world that everything he said was true. Based on his resurrection, then yes, he is the God who always is and was before time began. Out of God's free will, he took a human form, lived among humankind for thirty-three years, and taught us how to achieve godly consciousness by knowing the truth.

Through the life of Jesus, God has demonstrated to us that He is not just an aloof being high up there in His heavenly kingdom. He understands intimately what we are going through on earth. Jesus offered each human being his divine love from the cross, whether they believed in him or not; his offer is denied to no one. Through Jesus, God has done the utmost to reveal who He is and the relationship He wants to establish with humankind without taking away our freedom of choice. There is nothing more He could have done.

In a way, one might say that Jesus is exclusive because he is the one God who created the universe and everything in it. On the other hand, Jesus is inclusive because he offers to each one of us the way, the truth, and a new life in God's love.

JUDGMENT AND HELL

According to Christian understanding, Jesus took the punishment for sins on behalf of all people in all generations, and this is the basis for forgiveness. Because of what Jesus did, all sins are forgivable. All we have to do is ask for it and God will give us the chance for a new beginning, with no debt due to Him because Jesus has already paid it. What a deal! This is the new covenant Jesus established.

The big question is, how about those people who have never heard of Jesus or who believe in God but don't believe in Jesus? Can they be saved? My answer to this question is that, ultimately, it is God's prerogative to decide whom He forgives. We really don't know. My own experience tells me that it is not so cut-and-dried that those who are baptized as Christians are saved and others are condemned.

My mother-in-law died a non-Christian. I am sure she had heard of Jesus Christ at some point in her life, but as far as I know, she never became a Christian. She came to me in a vision when I was at a very low point in my life and comforted me. (See the story in chapter 8.) In the vision, she didn't say a word; she only smiled at me, and I felt instantly warm and comfortable. Many times in his teachings, Jesus told us there will be a separation of the righteous and wicked and that the evil ones will be cast outside into the darkness where there is "weeping and gnashing of teeth." My mother-in-law wasn't weeping or gnashing her teeth when I saw her in that vision.

My wife, Liena, also died a non-Christian. She and I were not churchgoing people at that time. Although I had been baptized when I was a child, as a young adult, I was turned off by the different Christian churches, each claiming that theirs was the right path and that the others were somewhat off course. My position was not to submit to any of them. Twenty years have passed since Liena's death, and I have felt so far that our relationship did not end with her death. For all this time, I have felt the positive energy from her spirit that has continued to be so nourishing and supportive in many expanded ways. That cannot be coming from, it seems to me, a godforsaken place of darkness, weeping, and gnashing of teeth.

How do I reconcile my experiences with the Christian interpretation that those who have not accepted Jesus during their lifetime on earth will go to hell? My current thinking is that heaven and hell are not so black and white. This one creator God who is the source of everything is far beyond human imagination and understanding. If God is more merciful than what He told us in the Bible, that does not render the Bible untrue.

Hell to me means separation from God's righteousness, mercy, and love; and the consequences of this separation can occur here on earth and extend into the next existence.

We all know what a life that is not righteous, merciful, and loving can lead to. One can become increasingly depressed, angry, and vengeful. God, in fact, does not punish us when we deviate from His guidance, but He allows the consequences of sins to play out. Actually, God does not send people to hell; the outcome is of our own making. Based on what Jesus did, we can say that God hates punishing people. He hates it so much that

He would rather take the punishment Himself on our behalf through Jesus. It is unthinkable that the sovereign God of the universe would go through so much trouble to show us His love.

In addition to the physical pain, the way Jesus was crucified was the most humiliating. The people hurled insults at him, they stripped him naked, "and they divided up his clothes by casting lots" (Luke 23:34). The paintings of the crucifixion always show a piece of cloth in his middle just to be respectful. Jesus volunteered to go through all that. He could have wiped out the whole world and started it all over.

There could be many reasons why Jesus made this choice. Two reasons to me are the most important. First, he wanted to finish his mission on earth—take the punishment for the sins of the world so that we could have a chance for a new life in God's mercy and love. Second, he wanted to preserve our spiritual freedom. God wants us to love him back out of our free will. To me, the message from Jesus's crucifixion is not "believe or I will send you to hell." The first words Jesus said after he was nailed on the cross were these: "Father, forgive them, for they do not know what they are doing" (Luke 23:34). *Them* in this message includes not only those who nailed him on the cross but also every human being through the end of time. Whether one believes in Jesus or not, no person is excluded from this statement. He knows each one of us by name and all the sins we will commit during our lifetime.

Through the crucifixion of Jesus, God did his utmost to demonstrate His mercy and love without making us His puppets. If we reject Jesus's offer of redemption, what are we rejecting? When we understand who Jesus is and what he went through to make this offer to us, it should really be an obvious choice on our part. What can be better than this new covenant from the one God who created everything in the vast universe yet knows each one of us intimately?

Some Christians believe that a person cannot enter heaven unless he or she was baptized, and so even an infant who died without being baptized would go to hell. This belief makes no sense to me. I cannot believe God would send my sister Mary, who lived only nine days, to hell had she not been baptized.

We all have a tendency to pass quick and superficial judgments on others. Jesus has a warning against judging in Luke 6:37: "Do not judge, and you will not be judged. Do not condemn, and you will not be condemned." God is the only perfect judge because He knows everything in a person's heart and mind; nothing can be hidden from Him. Jesus did provide a wider guideline on this "do not judge" message. He commanded us to use sound judgment by God's revealed standards in his words: "Do not judge by appearance, but judge with right judgment" (John 7:24 ESV).

Accepting Jesus's offer of salvation in baptism helps us understand what God's standards of righteousness are and His expectations of those who accept His grace of forgiveness. Jesus made it clear that his followers are expected to pass on God's grace to others and make the world a better place. Like Jesus, each Christian is called to be a shepherd in some ways. He also warned us of God's disposition of those who deviate from grace. Just like his promises of salvation deserve our total trust because of who Jesus is, his warnings are therefore just as real. God will ultimately separate good and evil, and the judgment by this highest wisdom and authority is perfect.

ETERNAL LIFE AND HEAVEN

I believe we are spiritual beings going through a temporal human experience. In other words, we are created to be everlasting. My body is only a vehicle during this earthly journey. Someday, I will get out of this vehicle and continue on.

Reading the story of the resurrected Jesus in the Bible gives me a picture of the next phase of my existence. After the biological phase, I will not be subject to any of the perils of life on Earth. I will not become injured, sick, or aged. I won't need to feed my body with food or make money to support my family. There will be no need to infringe on the possessions of others because there will be an abundance of everything. Anything I wish will be done, and anywhere I want to go, I will be at immediately. I can even be in multiple places at the same time.

Souls in the spiritual world can enjoy intimate relationships with anyone. There won't be any possessiveness because relationships won't take up someone's time or space. There is only joy, no one can get hurt, and gender takes on a different meaning. Above all, we all live in God's glory. Each soul carries a different aspect of God's infinite creativity and thus shines with unique brilliance.

Likewise, we can start experiencing some aspects of heaven here on earth too. Again, through what Jesus did, we know that God is and continues to be intimately involved with each one of us and the world. We feel good every time we experience godly nature—when we extend mercy and love to others or stand up for justice and the truth or become enlightened by wisdom. All the good things we experience here have ramifications beyond this world. The primary purpose of human life is an opportunity to get to know God.

Heaven after this human life means an existence in God's presence and love. There are two main religious and philosophical perspectives on afterlife. One is reincarnation, held by Buddhists; and the other is resurrection, held by Christians. The reincarnation model holds that people live through multiple lifetimes on earth in different bodies until the soul gets enlightened enough to take on spiritual form. I have given the subject of reincarnation a lot of thought; and my position is, first of all, earth is not a place where life-sustaining conditions are perpetual.

We know our sun will burn itself out someday and our Milky Way galaxy is escaping outward, along with millions or billions of other galaxies in the universe, from a center point from which they all came. The outward expansion is making the universe increasingly less dense as the galaxies move farther from one another at accelerating speeds. The implication of this progression is that the entire universe may eventually come to a cold ending when its density continues to drop and all energies burn out. This macro observation is telling me that everything within the time-space-matter world is temporal and part of a one-way journey. Perpetuity is, therefore, not in this state of nature but is in the source of it all—generally regarded as God.

So in the temporal world, there may come a time in the future when there is no more life to reincarnate into because the entire universe will have closed down and all forms of life will have ended. The resurrection model offers new life in God and perpetual enlightenment in Him. Therefore, there is no need to come back to earth in biological lives to find enlightenment. To me, the resurrection model is more appealing and makes sense.

WHAT IS THE POINT OF THINKING ABOUT ALL THESE THINGS?

Faith creates reality. "As you think, so shall it be!" is a saying passed on since ancient times. Dreams can come true if one works hard at them with passion. It can work the other way too: if someone holds a negative outlook on life, then life can be miserable for him.

We all have seen cases where a person's life seems to be a self-fulfilling prophecy. The story in the Bible tells us that the almighty God who created the universe is intimately involved with our daily lives; He loves each human being and wants to help us go through this treacherous earthly journey. The Bible verse I find profoundly inspiring in infinite ways is Psalm 46:10: "Be still, and know that I am God."

This message is telling us that God has a plan for everything and He is in control, yet the highest authority and power in the universe is most subtle and gentle. That is why the way to connect with God and be enlightened by His divine wisdom is through stillness, or solitude.

Of course, being calm is always a challenge for everyone. At this point in my life, I am still learning how to be better at letting go and being still. Jesus came into this world and promised that he would give us his divine assistance if we let him. Here are some of his messages:

> Come to me, all you who are weary and burdened, and I will give you rest. Take my yoke and learn from me, for I am gentle and humble in heart, and you will find rest in your souls. (Matt. 11:28–29)
>
> Ask and it will be given to you; seek and you will find; knock and the door will be opened to you. (Matt. 7:7)
>
> And surely I am with you always, to the end of the age. (Matt. 28:20)

For me, one of the most wonderful realizations about my consciousness is that it is expanding with my understanding of the truth—God's truth. Because God is infinite, my consciousness is infinite too. God created me, but He did not make me to be His puppet. Even though God has perfect foresight of the outcome of my life, it is the divine intent that I am a free spirit. God went through a great deal to tell me that. As a free spirit, I am a coauthor of my life story with God. What pleases me pleases Him and vice versa because we are one.

I am now in the last one-third of my time on earth. I want to make this the most significant third in terms of learning, growing, and doing things that hopefully make the world a better place in some small ways. In the last two chapters of this book, I summarize some of my goals and objectives in the precious time still available to me.

12

Who I Am and What to Do about It: Letting the Truth Sink In

Human life is a complicated journey. It really took the first two-thirds of it for me to learn the basic framework of who I am. Although the truth is simplistic, understanding it is no simple matter. The questions of who I am and who God is are always somewhat a mystery. From my point of view, the two questions are linked. This seems to be the divine intent; if there were no mystery, there would be no need for wisdom; motivation for scientific explorations; and inspiration for creative expressions through literature, art, and music.

It is true that I started learning about who I am through struggling with these mysteries. Although I don't expect to find complete answers, progress along this infinite path constantly reaffirms why I was given this life. As I take on this consciousness, my value in life becomes broader, deeper, and higher. I am part of that I am—the "I Am"' that created the universe and everything in it. It is in this expanding consciousness that happiness can be sustained regardless of the changes in life.

THE "NOW WHAT?" QUESTION

With all the truths I have learned about who I am and who God is, what are the implications for day-to-day living? Faith is not some kind of occasional esoteric high vision. It should be down-to-earth and real and serve as a consistent guide for every activity and all personal relationships in good times and bad. Like a compass, it always provides a sense of direction and frame of reference for making lifelong goals as well as daily plans.

Personally, I believe a life guided by faith seeks to glorify God and serve the world. Glorifying God does not necessarily mean engaging in church-related work, but it is a state of being that personifies all that is good, in all aspects of life. The world at large needs people of godly consciousness to serve it like raindrops that fall on the ground. Each drop of rain cleanses and nourishes wherever it falls. It appears to me that there is a unique purpose in each human life, and each stage of a lifetime can have a different focus and value.

Goals can be created and values developed through a God–human partnership. At my sixty-fifth year, it is necessary to ask what I want to do with the remainder of my time, which I know is rather limited—thirty years maybe, which, quite frankly, would be good enough. Hopefully, I will see the completion of the projects I care about and see my grandchildren grow up.

A major challenge for me going forward is the progressive decline in my eyesight that started noticeably after age fifty and has been happening at an increasing rate since age sixty. Now my right eye is almost totally blind, and my ability to see contrast through my left eye is diminishing. Since early 2011, I have needed to walk with a white cane when I go out, just to be safe. Going out at night is increasingly difficult, and I avoid it as much as possible.

Becoming totally blind sometime in the years ahead is a real possibility. At this time, the question for me is how to get the most out of my eyesight while I still have it. Fortunately, with the help of the latest technology, I am still effective doing computer work. I am using ZoomText, a screen-reading software that provides magnification, color, and voice options. With this software, there is still a lot I can do.

One thing I can do well is offer professional knowledge and expertise in business management to select nonprofit organizations serving societal causes that I care about. Having achieved financial independence, I am now free to provide pro bono management services to organizations of my choice. Even if I become totally blind, I will view that not as an obstruction but, rather, as a notice for me to do something different or do what I do differently. All through my life, it has been—and more so going forward, it will be—a matter of self-management and a process of establishing new purposes.

Actually, I started planning for this next occupation a few years before retiring in 2009 from my regular job at the Association of Bay Area Governments. With my declining eyesight, activities like traveling would not be my main focus in retirement. I have come to the realization that the value I create for others is a measure of the value of my own life. Thus, I intend to remain professionally active for as long as possible. Serving on boards of nonprofits would be the best way for me to offer my service, and additionally, this approach provides the flexibility of serving several organizations concurrently.

MY CURRENT CLIENT ORGANIZATIONS

LIGHTHOUSE FOR THE BLIND AND VISUALLY IMPAIRED OF SAN FRANCISCO

I started serving on the board of the LightHouse in June 2005. The LightHouse is a nonprofit organization with a mission of helping blind and visually impaired people to live independently. It provides rehabilitation services for vision loss, a low-vision clinic, and recreation and employment opportunities for people who are blind or visually impaired. The LightHouse also serves as a resource for matters relating to public policy. My interest in supporting this organization is, on one hand, providing it with management expertise and, on the other, learning about services available as my vision declines further. I also want to find inspiration from some of the highly accomplished blind and visually impaired people associated with the LightHouse.

The LightHouse is a rather complex organization. In addition to offering services related to vision loss, it has an exclusive contract with the Department of Defense to manufacture small tissue-paper packets for military use, typically placed in meals ready to eat (MREs). The LightHouse owns three hundred acres of land in Napa County, donated to it about sixty years ago. Now, the land is used as a campground for blind and visually impaired clients and their families to experience nature—the Enchanted Hills Camp provides numerous very popular training and recreational programs all year round.

The LightHouse's revenue sources include government grants, contracts, donations, bequests, fees for service, and investment income from an endowment fund. Since 2005, my significant contributions have included serving as board treasurer, chairing the Finance Committee and Investment Committee, participating in the search for a new executive director, and arranging in 2011 the financing for the purchase of a factory building in San Leandro and an office building on Market Street in San Francisco, which will be the new headquarters starting in 2015.

One important program the LightHouse offers is assistance to blind and visually impaired people in finding employment through training in writing résumés, interviewing, and using adaptive technology in the workplace. I have met many blind people among both board members and staff who are outstanding professionals in various fields of specialty. One young woman was particularly inspirational to me—Jessie Lorenz, who worked at the LightHouse as the director of public policy and information.

Jessie has been blind since birth. Once she said to me, "I don't know the meaning of *red*, but I am not missing anything. My life is full." When she said this, I thought, *How could she not be missing anything if she has never seen?* Jessie has a lot to teach me. She won a gold medal at the 2008 Paralympic Games held in Beijing, playing with the US Women's Goalball Team. After she returned from the games, she told me that standing at the award ceremony, listening to the national anthem play, was an experience she will never forget. Jessie also won a silver medal at the 2004 Athens Paralympic Games.

I began to understand that a person blind from birth relates to the world in a different way that sighted people don't see. Jessie has experienced something that I could never achieve and can tell me what it is like. Her story is another example of how each human life is unique and fascinating in potential. Jessie is now the executive director of the Independent Living Resource Center in San Francisco.

Goalball is a team sport designed for blind athletes, originally developed as a means to rehabilitate visually impaired World War II veterans. Opposing teams try to throw a ball with bells embedded in it into the opponents' goal. The sport evolved over the decades following and has been part of the Paralympics since 1980.

The LightHouse completed interior renovations of the top three floors of the building at 1155 Market Street in downtown San Francisco in 2016 and moved its headquarters there. One of the board members, Chris Downey, an architect who lost his eye sight in 2008, provided invaluable input in the interior design for blind and low-vision people. During the construction process, the LightHouse received a once-in-a-lifetime huge gift—a person in Seattle who became blind in the last few years of his life and had no prior connection with the San Francisco LightHouse passed away with a will designating the SF LightHouse as beneficiary of his estate, valued at $120 million.

With this new wealth, the new headquarters are equipped with state-of-the-art technology. To enhance the functionality of the space, the three floors are connected with a central staircase. There is a dormitory section to provide lodging for groups of people attending weeklong training classes. There is enough space for a teaching kitchen, an exercise room, a volunteers' center, a low-vision clinic, a boardroom with floor-to-ceiling windows overlooking the San Francisco Civic Center skyline, and many other amenities. The new wealth also enabled the LightHouse to finance the purchase of a majority interest of the lower eight floors of the building. These floors have been rented for many years to only one tenant—the City of San Francisco, housing a number of its administrative departments. Being the majority owner of the building, the LightHouse will have space for future expansion.

The LightHouse is a very different organization in 2020 than when I joined its board fifteen years ago. It is now professionally managed in every aspect of its operation, offering excellent services to the blind and low-vision community. One significant program started in early 2020 is manufacturing of cleaning products. A factory building across the Bay was purchased to house this production operation. It will provide many job opportunities for blind people. The LightHouse got into this business at the right time, right in the middle of the COVID-19 pandemic. Demand for these products has been good at the get go and is expected to continue after the pandemic passes.

I received a very special honor shortly after the LightHouse moved into its new headquarters on Market Street. They named the low-vision clinic located on the tenth floor the Joseph K. Chan Low Vision Clinic. I am a client of this clinic too. I have eye exams there to monitor my vision. It is a sweet feeling to be treated in a clinic that bears my name.

I received training at the LightHouse on using a number of computer and iPhone applications. These tools are extremely helpful to live independently and productively with low vision. The trainers who trained me are blind from birth, but they always astonish me with how good they are in using access technology. As they teach me new skills, they are also my inspiration.

For more information about the LightHouse in San Francisco, visit its website at www.lighthouse-sf.org.

OPERA PARALLÈLE OF SAN FRANCISCO

Music has always been my interest since I was a teenager. It is therapeutic and inspirational to me. As I grew older, I realized that music is an important part of humanity. I like what violinist Isaac Stern said in his movie *From Mao to Mozart*: "If more people liked music, the world would be a better place."

In 2006, the San Francisco Conservatory of Music moved to a new building on Oak Street, very conveniently located for me to get to after work. Attending concerts there became one of my favorite entertainments. Every year, students and faculty members perform hundreds of concerts at the conservatory. I particularly enjoy performances by young musical talents from all over the world.

In 2007, Nicole Paiement, director, conductor, and professor at the University of California–Santa Cruz, started the Ensemble Parallèle (EP, currently Opera Parallèle) with a mission to produce contemporary operas. Initially, the ensemble was housed at the conservatory, and I have attended a number of performances by Nicole and her contemporary music team. As its name implies, Ensemble Parallèle presents its operas in collaboration with multimedia artists, such as dancers, choreographers, and audiovisual specialists. These collaborations allow EP to reach wider and younger audiences.

In 2008, Ensemble Parallèle formed a board of directors in the process of becoming a professional opera company. I offered my support and was appointed by the board to be its first treasurer. To get the operation started, board members had to do hands-on work. My first task was to set up the accounting system using QuickBooks. My previous experience in accounting system design and implementation came in handy. Fortunately, the initial board had the right combination of people to take on various necessary tasks.

In its first three years, EP produced two works annually. In 2012, the board decided to change the company name to Opera Parallèle of San Francisco, and in the 2013 season, the Opera Parallèle produced three works. Opera Parallèle is gaining national acclaim. The 2012 production of *The Great Gatsby* won first prize in the National Opera Association's professional-division opera production competition. That was the second top award in two consecutive years. The production of *Orphee* also won first prize in 2011.

My involvement with Opera Parallèle broadened my interest in contemporary musical art. The people on the board come from different backgrounds and are committed to OP. I enjoy going to the performances and participating in the management team. Contemporary operas reflect issues in contemporary society. The OP team is offering opera lovers in the Bay Area and beyond intellectually stimulating operatic productions. In 2013, OP hired its first executive director and one part-time administrative staff. It is an honor and privilege for me to work with this talented team of people who love art and share a common vision in creating a revered artistic organization.

The COVID-19 pandemic in 2020 brought major disruptions to performing arts. All performances before a large audience have been cancelled. The performance of *Harvey Milk*, OP's production about the life of Harvey Milk, the first openly gay public official in California who was assassinated in 1978 while serving as supervisor of San Francisco, originally scheduled in May 2020 has been postponed. OP is committed to presenting the premiere of the opera *Harvey Milk* soon, hopefully sometime next year.

After completing my full term as a member of the OP board, I continued serving as a volunteer in its Finance Committee. My interest is to assist OP in financial matters. Artistic organizations typically operate with tight budgets. The COVID-19 pandemic brought on an extraordinary challenge as live performances are cancelled. Nevertheless, the best will survive. OP will; it produces art that people value. In this generation, as the world is polarized with so much discourse, performing arts should be part of the solution. Arts reflect the humanity that all people share deep down.

For more information about Opera Parallèle, visit www.operaparallele.org.

CALIFORNIA PUBLIC AGENCIES SELF-DIRECTED TAX-ADVANTAGED RETIREMENT SYSTEM (STARS)

STARS is a trust established to administer deferred compensation plans on behalf of local government entities within the state of California. The key differences between STARS and the other plans in the market are that STARS is transparent in disclosing fees charged by service providers of the plan; sponsoring agencies have the option of participating in the governance of STARS by electing a representative to be a member of the board of trustees; and personal investment assistance is available to each participating employee at no extra management fee. In addition, the service providers engaged by the STARS board operate with declining fee schedules based on total assets in the pool. As total assets grow, fees will be lower.

The primary objective in offering the STARS plan is to give the public-sector employees an alternative to the many hidden fees charged by other plans in the market, and in the long run, the best interest of the investors will be served. The board of trustees engaged two partners that believe in the same philosophy in managing retirement assets, Unified Trust Company and SageView Financial Advisors. Both partners are highly qualified and reputable in this business and have been willing to help grow the pool from its inception.

UTC serves as the discretionary trustee and is fully responsible for setting investment policies and selection of appropriate investment options. Sponsoring public employers thereby pass their fiduciary responsibility to the discretionary trustee. This is another significant advantage of the STARS program.

I worked on creating the STARS program before I retired from the Association of Bay Area Governments. Herbert Pike, my successor at ABAG; Richard Averett, executive director of Regional Government Services; and I came up with the initial design of the program, organized a board of trustees, and began operation on September 1, 2009, with two agencies and about $3 million in assets. To give the plan my continued support, I stayed on the board after my retirement from ABAG and have been serving as board secretary. Our goal is to make STARS a standard retirement investment–management plan for public agencies in California. It will take some time to gain recognition and build reputation.

After six years in operation, although the pool has grown in number of participants and total assets under management, the number of agencies in STARS had not increased. The board realized that it is time for a reorganization and started looking for another service provider. MassMutual replaced UTC as service provider effective on April 1, 2017. MassMutual has more agents in California and is more capable in delivering in-person and online services to STARS agencies and participants. SageView stayed on as financial advisor and assumed additional responsibilities of investment selection and a full fiduciary.

In July 2020, the board approved a new public agency joining STARS. Another agency is interested in the STARS program and is going through review with its management. The board also approved allocating resources for STARS staff to focus on marketing the program going forward.

For more information about STARS, visit www.starsca.org.

LUTHERAN CHURCH OF THE HOLY SPIRIT

In chapter 11, I shared the story of the midlife turning point in my consciousness, and the impetus of this change was the realization that humility is the foundation of wisdom.

Notwithstanding the issues I have with organized religion, particularly with Christian churches, I felt that it was necessary for me to reexamine Christianity.

First of all, I wanted to know the subject matter in more depth so that I could provide educated answers for myself, and although I know there is no such thing as a perfect church, I wanted to go to one and see whether I could benefit from the experience and have something positive to contribute at the same time. There are many churches close to my house. The one that is most convenient to me is the Lutheran Church next to Safeway, where I get my groceries.

In the early part of 2003, I started going to this church. My first impression was that the people there were quite friendly. In addition to worship services, I began participating in a number of activities, such as Bible classes and fellowship gatherings. Over the years, I definitely have expanded my biblical knowledge. Pastors Shiu-ming Lau and Christopher Ng emphasize application of biblical teachings to real life. I agree with their approach. The main benefits I got early on from this church were not only interpretations of the Bible but also the opportunity to become better at listening to other people's points of view and telling them mine.

There were challenges in this church experience. It didn't take long for me to notice that there was no transparency in financial matters. The church did not publish comprehensive financial reports for the congregation. For example, assets and liabilities of the church were not reported.

For a number of years, the church had been engaging in fundraising for the construction of a new church building and had accumulated a couple million dollars in the building fund. On many occasions, I advised the church council that with the amount of money in this church, compliance with professional accounting and reporting standards was necessary for the protection of both the congregation and the church officers. My recommendations gradually fell to the sideline, partly because the attitude was that professional accounting standards were for the secular world and not applicable to churches. My advice was that these standards were part of good financial stewardship in any human organization, religious or secular.

Another stumbling block in making changes was that the people serving in the church council at that time did not have the capacity to implement professional accounting standards, and so the deficiency continued. In the last quarter of 2011, head elder Barron Fong asked me if I would accept a nomination to serve in the next church council. I answered that if I took on the task, things would be very different; I was not sure whether the church was ready for change, but it was worth a try. The election took place in November 2011, and the congregation voted me in for a three-year term beginning January 2012.

My first task was a review of the condition of the church's financial records. At this time, my eyesight has deteriorated to the point that I no longer can read printed text, but with software for low vision, I am still efficient in reading the computer screen. This process included doing extensive coding corrections for transactions improperly recorded over the preceding three years. I spent a whole month doing that, which was not surprising. What I wasn't prepared for was the condition of the accounting records for an afterschool tutorial program.

Its bank account hadn't been reconciled for eighteen months, and certain income deposits had not been recorded, which meant the church didn't know whether the program had been profitable in the past two years or whether any money was missing. I realized that I needed someone qualified to clean up the set of books for this program while I worked on the general fund set of books; otherwise, there would be a substantial delay in the preparation of the 2011 year-end financial reports. Fortunately, one member of the church, Ann Truong, who is a CPA, stepped forward. With both of us collaborating, we finished the year-end close and presented the full set of 2011 financial reports to the congregation in February 2012.

Another fiscal matter I needed to resolve was the spread of some rumors that the church building under construction was running overbudget and costing as much as $5 million. Lack of transparency hatches rumors that usually are exaggerations or not true. The church building was completed in the early part of 2012 and was put into service in April. As soon as all the construction costs were paid, I did a full report of the building costs and presented it to the congregation. Based on generally accepted accounting principles, the new building costs totaled $3.5 million and were within the construction budget. That is how far off from the truth rumors can be. What this church has experienced underscores the fact that when sound fiscal management practices are not being followed, it may hurt the spirit and hamper the mission of spreading the Gospel.

In accepting this position on the church council, I had a personal agenda—intending to implement during my term accounting policies and procedures that are appropriate for church operation. But the real challenge is whether they will be upheld after I leave office. If it works only while I am serving, I will not consider my work successful. Essentially, the culture has to change to recognize the value of sound fiscal management. So far, progress has been good; members of the finance committee and the church council have been supportive. Continuity and succession planning have to be addressed going forward.

This church is not unusual in its struggle with fiscal management issues. In 2010, Barron Fong invited me to participate in an accounting research project initiated by the Lutheran Church California-Nevada-Hawaii (CNH) District. The objective of this initiative was to identify the fiscal management challenges among the approximately 180-member churches in the three-state district and develop appropriate training programs for church officers and staff. The first task of the Accounting Research Committee was sending out a survey to study the accounting practices of member churches.

Based on the information collected, 39 percent of the churches were not using accounting software applications that can generate professional financial reports. In response to the needs reflected by the survey, the Accounting Research Committee offered in January 2011 a fiscal management seminar for CNH District member churches with topics including guidelines for treasurers, IRS filings, employee benefits, and insurance needs for churches. It was well attended by about eighty representatives from thirty churches. This research and training initiative has raised awareness of the range of fiscal management issues and of the CNH District as a resource center for member churches.

What does the Bible say about compliance with professional accounting standards? Following generally accepted accounting principles (GAAP) is a way to ensure integrity. Although GAAP may evolve over the ages, integrity does not change and is always required. Here are a couple of Bible messages about integrity:

> Whoever walks in integrity walks securely, but whoever takes crooked paths will be found out. (Prov. 10:9)
>
> The integrity of the upright guides them, but the unfaithful are destroyed by their duplicity. (Prov. 11:3)

The practical implication of these messages is that every human organization, religious or secular, intending to stay on the path of continued success must follow applicable legal, professional, and ethical standards. Otherwise, it will eventually break down and fall apart at some point.

I left the church at age twenty-five and was not a member of any church for thirty years because I was turned off by organized religion. My return was driven by the realization that human flaws do not tarnish Jesus's teachings; they only underscore the enormous challenge in truly living up to his standards. It is a higher calling for me to offer my services to improve the church's effectiveness in spreading the Gospel than to stay away from church. No church can be a perfect organization as long as it is a congregation of people. In the church I am attending, I want to represent a voice of reason, and a voice of reason is the voice of Christ. Nothing is special about what I do because each Christian is supposed to be a spokesperson for Christ and bring the fruit of his work to not only Christian communities but also the larger secular world.

In 2014, the church decided to offer a preschool in the local community. There are very few Christian preschools in the neighborhood. The plan is to remodel a building the church owns down the street, fourteen blocks away, to make it suitable for a preschool operation. An organizing committee was formed to move the plan forward. I volunteered to serve in the committee. The process turned out to be very challenging every step of the way—in finalizing the architectural design, getting the city's planning department approval, finding a contractor through competitive bidding, and fundraising. The most challenging phase, however, is not building the facility or raising the money; it is finding the teaching staff.

In our recruitment process, we realized that the well-qualified teachers already had jobs and were reluctant to take the chance of a new preschool. Finally, the Help-U-Grow Preschool managed to open for business in July 2019 with three students. Over the next several months, the growth in enrollment was far less than expected, and the cash reserve continued to drain and was running out soon. We realized that the situation called for a reorganization.

Around that time, the COVID-19 pandemic was sweeping across the world like a tsunami. The City of San Francisco issued a shelter-in-place order, closing down office buildings, restaurants, and schools. We closed the HUG Preschool on March 16, 2020, in response. We took the opportunity to execute the reorganization plan and put a new team in place.

A few weeks later, recognizing childcare centers as one of

the essential businesses, the city allowed preschools to operate under specific safety guidelines. The HUG Preschool reopened on June 15, 2020, and was given a maximum enrollment of twelve students. Under such a restriction, we can barely breakeven financially. Fortunately, we received help from the government. To relieve economic hardships caused by the COVID-19 pandemic, Congress passed the CARES Act which includes the Payroll Protection Program (PPP) loan to assist small businesses to keep their employees on the payroll. Our church applied and received $34,000 of PPP loan, which will be forgiven if used on payroll. This is like a gift from heaven. It will help sustain our operation until enrollment builds up to twelve students.

In my personal view, the HUG Preschool is going through a challenging beginning but now well positioned to be a good school. I envision the church will continue to operate this preschool for decades to come, offering little children a nurturing start of education. I am fortunate to have the opportunity to participate in setting up its accounting system and establishing sound administrative policies. I have to acknowledge the assistance from Ann Truong, a practicing CPA and CFO, who has been working with me on the financial matters of this church since 2012. She is more proficient with the QuickBooks online accounting system and more current with best management practices than I am.

For more information about the Lutheran Church and the HUG Preschool, visit www.lcholyspirit.org and www.hugpreschool.com.

ANOTHER NEW ROLE FOR ME

In 2012, I became the proud grandfather of two wonderful baby boys. Haven was born on February 1 to April and Joey, and Nathaniel was born on March 30 to Kevin and Marla. Both are adorable babies, and they bring great joy to everyone in the family. On August 28, 2013, I was blessed again with my third grandchild, a girl this time, from Kevin and Marla. They call her Betsy. I am elated. They are not done yet. On October 14, 2016, Caleb was born to Kevin and Marla; and on March 23, 2018, Pearce was born to April and Joey. We are incredibly blessed.

There are some differences between being a father and being a grandfather. First of all, I am not directly responsible for raising my grandchildren. That is my children's responsibility. I only give a helping hand whenever I can. When I first became a father, perhaps I was too busy working and making money to feed the family, and I tended to take things for granted. As a grandfather, since I have more time to think, I don't want to take anything for granted.

How these babies grow is nothing short of a miracle. For the first few months, all they eat is breast milk, and they grow really fast. There is no scientific explanation of how breast milk disseminates into bones, muscles, hair, and skin. What kind of intelligence does it take to make that happen? Whatever it is, it is far beyond us. This is just another piece of evidence that God's creation work has never stopped since the very beginning, and He has to be intimately involved in bringing new life into the world.

What do I want my role to be as a grandfather? I love spending time with my grandchildren and watching them grow. Since we are not living together, I try to go to them and stay a few days as often as I can. Sometimes, they come to visit me. Playing with them is my great joy. I become one of them, and we make up our own games. Hide-and-seek and catching one another are so much fun once again.

One big obstacle that keeps me from doing as much as I want with my grandchildren is my declining eyesight. As their angelic faces become increasingly blurry and dim, I feel like I want to cry. All through my life, I have been trained to find alternatives to get around obstacles, but there is no way to get around this one. I can give up seeing everything else, but not being able to see my grandchildren is by far the most difficult possibility to accept. This challenge really underscores that there are lessons to learn at every stage of life, and yes, some new insights are coming to light.

First of all, God did not promise me any grandchildren. I am incredibly blessed to have them. My grandchildren are growing fast; they won't be babies all the time. In the blink of an eye, they will become kids, teenagers, and young adults. My declining eyesight makes time spent with them even more precious. They are blessings to me, and I should enjoy them as much as I can. These babies are teaching me something important, just by being here.

Despite my not being able to see them clearly, there are special things I can do for my grandchildren. Aside from being an occasional babysitter, contributing to their college trust funds, loving them, and giving advice are some of the things I can do well. On one hand, I am concerned that my grandchildren will face perils of human life in this dangerous world, on the other hand, with nurturing parents and good education, I believe they will grow up to be productive individuals and their life journeys will benefit the world. I'd like my grandchildren to know my life story, and hopefully, they will read this book someday.

SHAPING THE FUTURE

Life is all about managing changes, but facing the changes that are beyond one's control always presents the greatest difficulty. One of the big lessons I have learned is that everything about human life is temporary. All our bodily functions decline with age; and eventually, they all stop, and we say goodbye to the world. It seems to me we really have only two options in responding to such a prognosis—complain and feel sad or make the best out of it and have peace with the process. I cannot speak for everyone, but the second option has been my choice, time and time again.

Even though there are many changes in life that are not in my control, how I respond to them is up to me. As I give life changes my own touch, always doing my best gives me self-satisfaction, and I feel gratitude for having the experience. My fundamental belief is that the universe and humankind were created out of love, and love is revealed and demonstrated in so many ways through pain and suffering, through sacrifice and service. My purpose in life, therefore, is to maximize receiving and giving love. This is what I call the "God–me partnership" in writing the story that has yet to come.

For the rest of my time on earth, I see myself continuing to work on societal causes that are close to my heart. As I pass the term limits in the various boards on which I am currently serving, I will offer my service to other organizations, most likely in blindness rehabilitation and research, performing arts, education, and support of disadvantaged children. On my final day on this planet, I want to feel that I have been fully used. As life transpires before me, every twist and turn is a new beginning, at any age.

As I am living through this COVID-19 pandemic of 2020 that is bringing so much suffering to the world in many ways, one news report disturbed me deeply. The report indicated that the number of reported child abuse is down significantly. Since many of the child abuse cases are reported by school teachers, the children who are facing abusive situations at home could be suffering even more severe abuses as schools across the country are closed. To me, this is heart-breaking reality.

I know from my own childhood experience that children, especially in their early years, are not in the position to seek help. We know many children around the world are suffering in ways that affect the rest of their lives. The wellbeing of children has always been close to my heart. The four nonprofit organizations I currently am working with benefit children, directly and indirectly. To those beyond my work, I send financial support to organizations that help children; and to those beyond my financial support, I send my prayers.

13

Some Concluding Thoughts

THE HIGHEST PURPOSE

I believe the highest purpose of my life is not a program prescribed by an almighty God whose will is done on earth as it is in heaven, but, rather, it is jointly created by God and me. God's role in this partnership is to give me a framework, and my role is to set certain goals and fulfill them. God provided me with a body that I find as I wake up every morning, born on January 7, 1948, on planet Earth, as part of the Chan family genealogy, visually impaired and capable of understanding, feeling, and making choices. These are some of the factors that are God-given.

One important realization in my experience is that God did not get me started and then leave. He also has provided guidance and encouragement along this journey. As I step into the last one-third of my time on earth, the purpose of this partnership is becoming increasingly clear. In the concluding chapter of this book, I want to recap what has made this joint venture remarkable and what I look forward to.

The first thing that comes to mind when I think about what makes my story remarkable is how I overcame the stigma put on me when I was a child with the intention of loving protection.

The path to learning the truth was a long and painful one, but I persevered. Ironically, the one person who helped me the most along this path, my dear wife, Liena, also suffered painful experiences that were unintended consequence of loving family protection.

When we met, she and I had gone through different kinds of painful experiences; but we learned from them, persevered, and benefited from each other's knowledge and insights. How we met was clearly not my arrangement. I attribute that to a higher power. Our part was making the best of the opportunity to experience a loving relationship as husband and wife. This relationship transformed me and also blessed me with wonderful children and grandchildren. Whereas life and death are always the Creator God's business, my role is to determine what kind of person, parent, and grandparent I want to be.

Life is a learning work in progress. The pain, suffering, weaknesses, and frailties are opportunities to learn and grow—that is the godly intention in me. If there is one most important lesson I have learned in my life, I would say it is the realization that God does not create anything that is defective or junk. Defectiveness is only a human point of view; everything is here for a purpose.

Through vision loss, I have learned that there are three kinds of visions—eyesight, the vision that sees physical things; mental vision, our imagination that enables us to figure out how things work; and spiritual vision, the ability to understand the deeper and higher values in life. Clearly, my declining eyesight has contributed to the sharpening of my other two visions. I don't mean to say that every human being's challenges can be resolved in a positive way, but I have been inspired by the stories of many people who left behind great legacies, despite formidable obstacles in their lives.

New knowledge and insight carry new responsibilities, not only for me and my family but also for the larger world out there. To fulfill the highest purpose, my full potential, I have had to first persevere through the obstacles and tragedies. In my life story, God seems to have fulfilled His promise to help even though I didn't recognize it for most of my adult life. "So do not fear, for I am with you; do not be dismayed, for I am your God," Isaiah 41:10 reminds us. Jesus elaborated further on this message by explaining who we are, our relationship with him, and our relationship with our fellow people in these words: "I am the vine, you are the branches" (John 15:5). In this message, he is saying we are one continuous piece with him, and since he is one with the Father, we are one with the Father God too; God established His rule in the world, and our role is to spread out and distribute the fruit of His work to make the world a better place. As I advance through the different stages of life, I am still finding new meanings in these messages.

FULFILLMENT

I need to address one big issue in the conclusion of this book. It seems to me that all the events and lessons in life are in preparation for this one fundamental challenge—mortality. What is the meaning of happiness and success after all when life itself is temporal?

In my view, only my body is temporal; the knowledge and insights I have accumulated will have ramifications beyond my biological life. My mother is one person who inspired me with the way she faced mortality as it approached and the way she died. When she had her first heart attack in 2001, right after we celebrated her eightieth birthday, we rushed to the hospital to give her support and comfort. That's what we intended, but that wasn't the way it turned out. It went the other way around.

When I said to her, "I'll stay here with you," my mom said, "Go away. I am having a good time with the young and handsome doctors. You serve no useful purpose here. Go back to work." With an oxygen tube in her nose and an IV inserted in her vein, my mother kicked me in the butt and made me calm down. This is the attitude I want to have in the final hour of my time on earth. Her calmness and grace came from her faith and her acceptance of the process of human life and the realization that she had done the best she could with it. She went on to live almost ten more years after that incident and died on April 12, 2011. My brother Louis found her that day in her bed; she had passed away hours earlier.

Officers from the coroner's office came to pick up her body; and as they removed her blanket, we saw that in her right hand, she was holding a rosary, as if she was still praying with it. What a peaceful scene that was! Obviously, she had passed away quickly without any pain; otherwise, she would have reached for the phone or her pills. In a way, I took comfort in the knowledge that she received such a huge blessing. My mother had done the best she could for every person she had met, and God must have been very pleased with her life.

There are many other historical figures whose deeds benefited their fellow people during their lifetime and continue to inspire future generations after their passing. Consider Galileo Galilei (1564–1642), the Italian scientist who was put under house arrest by church authorities for the rest of his life for teaching his observation that the earth orbits around the sun. Such a concept was considered inconsistent with the scriptures.

Galileo was a religious person; his position was that science did not contradict the Bible, but interpretation of the Bible needed to be broader. Back in those days, only the clergy had the authority to interpret the Bible, and the general population had to accept the church's official interpretation. In his senior years, Galileo continued doing scientific research and publishing his findings despite becoming blind due to an eye infection. From my point of view, Galileo's contribution was not only new knowledge in astronomy but also a new perspective in interpretation of the Bible.

Another person who inspires me is Ludwig van Beethoven (1770–1827), a crucial figure in music whose compositions are immortal and loved by people around the world. Starting at about age thirty, he faced progressive hearing loss. For a concert pianist, that must have been devastating. He eventually had to give up performing and conducting and then focused on composing. Ironically, some of his best works were composed when he was almost totally deaf. Beethoven reflected this human struggle and triumph over fate in his music. His Symphony No. 5 opens with four-note short-short-short-long motif repeated twice to represent the knocking of fate. Remarkably, Beethoven uses this short-short-short-long motif again in the final movement of the symphony, with the brass instruments leading the theme in a striking, triumphant perseverance over fate.

Another well-known composition by Beethoven is his Symphony No. 9, completed in 1824, also known as "the choral symphony." Some people regard this work as the most important piece of music ever composed. Beethoven used human voice in the final movement to reflect the sanctity of the human spirit. The lyrics came from the poem "Ode to Joy" written by Friedrich Schiller in 1785. This was Beethoven's last symphony, and when it was first performed in Vienna on May 7, 1824, Beethoven was totally deaf.

Even though he was present, he couldn't hear it, but he did get on stage to acknowledge the thunderous applause from the audience, some of whom had tears in their eyes. Symphony No. 9 is probably the most performed piece of music and has been used as the theme song for many international activities. After the 1989 earthquake in the Bay Area that killed dozens of people, Herbert Blomstedt conducted the San Francisco Symphony and Chorus in a performance of the "Ode to Joy" at Golden Gate Park to lift the spirit of the citizens. I was there.

An important purpose of life is to fulfill one's full potential. Every person's potential is different. In reviewing my life story, I can see that the purpose of my life has changed over time, with each stage. Each stage has presented different challenges and learning opportunities. Which stage have I liked the most?

I would say the last stage that I am in right now is the most interesting. This is the stage in which I have the most freedom in giving back to serve the causes I care about.

One of the most encouraging lessons is that my declining eyesight will not hold me back from achieving what I want to do. As always, it only prompts me to find new ways and purposes. There could be other circumstances in the future that might entice me to change course such as being diagnosed with cancer, Alzheimer's, or Parkinson's or encountering some other unpredictable events. Since everything in life is temporary, there is an urgency to get the most done while I am still able. The uncertainty makes life more interesting and valuable. If there were no uncertainties, mysteries, or risks—then life could be boring and worthless because we wouldn't need to think.

Behind the perplexing dichotomies in human life is the inexhaustible love and wisdom from which all things were created. The value of my life is not measured by how much I have done, but it is in my having done the best I could to understand the divine intention of which I am part and to make a difference in the world in response to this understanding. This is how I would like to feel at my final hour.

With this frame of mind, the day I die should be the happiest day of my life—when all that I am committed to doing has been fulfilled and with all the love I have given and received, I will welcome the beginning of the next adventure.

Acknowledgments

First of all, I have to acknowledge my parents' contributions to this book. In the later part of my father's life (he passed away in 1998), he wrote a brief history of the Chan family covering about 140 generations and tracing our history back more than four thousand years. Chapter 1 is a summary of his records. My mother provided me with a lot of detailed information about the most recent three generations of this family tree, particularly what she and my father went through during the World War II years and their lives thereafter. I was fortunate enough to have recorded her recollections before her death in 2011.

One of my high school classmates, Stephen Chan, helped me in reading the first drafts of my manuscript. As one of the eyewitnesses to some of the challenges I had faced in school, he found my book interesting and gave me many suggestions. April and Kevin both shared with me memories of their childhood, teenage, and college years and how they felt about growing up with me and Liena. I certainly have learned a lot from raising them.

My niece Karen, daughter of my brother Louis, read my manuscript as I finished each chapter and gave me comments and suggestions. My brother-in-law Eric Chen, Liena's youngest brother, helped me in using Google Translate to find the Chinese names of cities in China. Another brother-in-law, Jason Ho, the husband of Liena's sister Eva, showed me how to look up Chinese characters using the Apple iPhone 5. These tools were very helpful in writing the Chinese names of people and places in chapter 1.

For chapter 9, covering my twenty-six-year career at the Association of Bay Area Governments, I talked with a number of my colleagues, many of whom have retired, to refresh my memories of certain historical events at ABAG. My son-in-law, Joseph Goodman, who runs a publishing company as a side business, gave me valuable advice about publishing a book. My dear friend Cathryn Hilliard helped me with the book summary for the back cover and website. While I was visiting over the Memorial Day weekend in 2014, my daughter-in-law, Marla, took the front cover picture for me on a natural trail near their house, as my son, Kevin, kept the kids entertained.

Finally, I have to acknowledge the Father God, the giver of life, who gave me this body and consciousness to explore and cocreate with Him what human life can be for me. One important lesson I have learned in the process of writing this book is that although it is my autobiography, it is also part of His big story too. I realized that He cries with me through pain and suffering and rejoices with me as I learn and grow spiritually. I am grateful for this opportunity of life as a human being.

www.ingramcontent.com/pod-product-compliance
Lightning Source LLC
Chambersburg PA
CBHW051149120626
46547CB00012B/1011